to tell The Truth

to tell The Truth

Some biblical guidelines to help Christians talk about the Faith

H.J.Appleby

Grace Publications Trust

GRACE PUBLICATIONS TRUST
139 Grosvenor Avenue
London N5 2NH
England

Joint Managing Editors:
J.P.Arthur M.A.
H.J Appleby

ISBN 0946462 429

Distributed by:
EVANGELICAL PRESS
12 Wooler Street
Darlington
Co Durham DL1 1RQ
England

Bible quotations, unless otherwise indicated, are taken from the New Revised Standard Version, published by the Oxford University Press. © 1989

Cover design by: HJA; some New Testament words describing how believers talked about the Faith

Art work by: Evangelical Press

Printed in Great Britain by The Bath Press, Somerset

To EILEEN
Wife, mother, grandmother, critic, comforter, colleague, who is
as responsible as I that this book has now appeared.

The question is ...

how is it possible to change,
so continuing to be relevant,
while remaining the same,
so as continuing to be Christian?

(The changing continuity of Christian Ethics: R.E.O.White)

To a superficial glance, the Rev. Martin Cleves is the plainest and least clerical looking of the party; yet, strange to say, *there* is the true parish priest, the pastor beloved, consulted, relied on by his flock; a clergyman who is not associated with the undertaker, but thought of as the surest helper under a difficulty, as a monitor who is encouraging rather than severe. Mr Cleves has the wonderful art of preaching sermons which the wheelwright and the blacksmith can understand; not because he talks condescending twaddle, but because he can call a spade a spade, and knows how to disencumber ideas of their wordy frippery.

(Scenes of clerical life: George Eliot*)*

Contents

Foreword

The problems and challenges of communication across cultures are nicely illustrated in Eugene Nida's lovely story of a taxi driver in India who was asked by a man when the service in a nearby church would end. 'I don't know', he said, 'but there are always four noises and there have been two so far this morning'.

I suspect that John Appleby's deep concern with this subject originated during his service among the Tamil people of India. Cross-cultural mission, especially when it is done in a culture shaped by the Hindu world view, raises the issues dealt with here in a most dramatic and unavoidable way. Later, when the author's commitment to the Great Commission led him to develop a ministry involving radio programming, the need to study communications theory and utilize modern insights into the processes by which messages are sent and received was certainly underlined again.

Many of us have reason to thank God that John Appleby did his homework so well. I still recall a seminar convened by the Grace Baptist Association of Churches (SE) and the Grace Baptist Mission many years ago to introduce the ideas outlined in this book. It was during those sessions that I was first alerted to the enormous importance of this subject. Later, during mission service in Nigeria, the lessons learned from John Appleby proved their worth over and over again. I am still utilizing these principles today as, in teaching a new generation of preachers and witnesses, I insist that urgent and serious attention be given to the need for effective, relevant and powerful communication.

The great thing about this book is that it holds in balance two principles that, alas, are often separated. First, the author insists that we must be faithful to the Bible. His concern to test everything by Scripture is evident throughout these pages. Second, he is equally concerned to challenge readers to an apostolic boldness in moving out from the sub-culture of the church and taking the Word of Life into the world. I endorse both these calls wholeheartedly. Relevance without faithfulness leads to compromise and spiritual death. However, many of us may be more in need of the warning that faithfulness without a willingness to take ground-breaking initiatives to ensure the transmission of the message to ever new hearers is also a path to extinction. Tragically, many churches have died even as their members have continually assured each other of their faithfulness.

John Appleby's excellent introduction to Christian communication helps us to face the challenge stated so well by Eugene Nida: 'Anyone communicating the Christian message must make certain that rejection of it is based upon a comprehension of the message, and not upon its incredible and irrelevant formulation'. Christians who are concerned to become workers 'who need not be ashamed' will find much help and stimulus in these pages, and I trust that this book will be widely read, pondered and acted upon.

David Smith
Principal, Northumbria Bible College

Preface

I realise now that this book has been in gestation a very long time; more than fifty years in fact. I remember still the sense of unease I often felt as a young teenager and member of the Strict Baptist Open-air Mission, when called upon to choose and read a Bible passage on street corners or village greens. This unease was not at being so publicly identified as a 'Bible basher' but at realising — even then — that so often what I read would not have been understood by any who might have heard.

The 'Ho ... come ... buy ... eat ... why spend money for what is not bread?' of Isaiah 55 (A.V.) would probably have conveyed something to my listeners (and sometimes there were some in those days!); but whatever would they make of 'the sure mercies of David' of verse 3? This sort of problem bothered me repeatedly. And the fairly common practice of using 'Gospel shots' as they were termed, where each person round the circle called out a verse from the Bible, left me wondering (for I did it like everyone else) whether this was really the way to use Scripture, as a kind of random 'magic' machine-gun fire.

Going out to work and then serving in the Fleet Air Arm during the Second World War produced what seemed a convenient solution to the problem: a dichotomy in my thinking where the comfort of my faith to myself was one thing and the spread of it in the world was quite another, but which was much less important to me. After the war, three years of theological study in the Strict Baptist Bible Institute were a delight to the former, and not too much involved with the latter. After all, one was seeking to prepare for ministry in 'our beloved denomination', as it was sometimes called, not in the big wide world. Yet, mercifully, 'the world' remained a disturbing niggle.

Completing my years at the Bible Institute, I received a call from a church in North London to serve as their pastor and happily did so for four years. They were formative years for me; my five deacons were both wise and gracious in guiding their young pastor. Yet the need of the wider mission field still remained an insistent niggle. I had several close links with missionaries serving with the Strict Baptist Mission in South India (now Grace Baptist Mission) which eventually became the channel of the Lord's irresistible voice to me. My church treasurer then had the tricky task of helping me to lay down the pastorate of his church and to take up the vocation of missionary work with the SBM — of which he was also the treasurer!

Arriving in India in 1952 (to serve among the established Tamil Baptist Churches where the thinking was already developing that the evangelising of Indians should be done by Indians, not by foreigners) brought a shock. I was in a non-Christian culture, struggling with a language which sometimes didn't even have the words that expressed my personal theological delights. And those to whom I had come were immersed in a society whose thinking was alien to biblical thought, and whose eastern methods of reasoning found the clear-cut absolutes of Graeco-Roman logic somewhat strange.

For instance, I recall sitting on a stone wall one day talking about God with a Tamil farmer. 'That stone is god', he said confidently. 'It cannot be', I replied with my best Aristotelian logic, 'for it is a stone'. 'Ah', he said, 'it is both a stone and god; everything is god. Don't you understand?' I did not! To me a stone was a stone and God was God. But how could what I had to say make sense in the context of his centuries-old patterns of thought?

Moving in 1958 to the production of Tamil Christian radio programmes for the Far East Broadcasting Company was another shock to the system. Now I was confronted with the problems of trying to prepare material intelligible to an audience I couldn't even see, let alone know. Anyone, anywhere in India (as letters began to indicate), could be listening now! Whatever could be done to make radio broadcasting a viable method of spreading the Christian message among the burgeoning millions of the Far East, whose own beliefs of salvation by religious ceremony could bring them no assured hope of heaven for they could never know if enough ceremonies had been performed.

Thus began the great search: how has God communicated? How did the apostles do it? What did the early church do about it? How did the Reformation message spread so fast? How has the message spread in Revival times? What has secular scientific research discovered? What research has been done in cross-cultural communication? Returning home finally in 1970 made it abundantly clear to me that Christians in the U.K. were no longer living in a nominally Christian country, not only because of our new pluralistic society but also because of the general loss of basic Christian understanding in our own nation; so communication here also needed to be cross-cultural, perhaps as never before.

This book is an attempt to distil some of the results of my simple research into short chapters of practical information, hopefully to stimulate wider concern, thought and prayer about the matter of our responsibility as believers rightly to represent the God we profess to worship and serve. For that reason I have written with 'ordinary' believers in mind (what child of God can really be described as 'ordinary'?) and with the hope that interest in the subject will not be confined to a few enthusiasts.

Over the years I have benefited from helpful discussion with a number of friends; not least among them the late David Everitt, Dr Jack Hoad, Clifford Pond, Frank Ellis and others; I have learned from the opportunity to read papers and studies passed on to me by such as Professor D.A.Carson, Dr David Smith, Professor Paul Helm, as well as gleaning from a wide variety of books and conferences, both Christian and secular. I should also gratefully record the helpful suggestions I have received from G.P.T. readers' panel members and from my editorial colleague, J.P.Arthur. The book is the better for their advice.

No man is truly original and doubtless I have been influenced by many comments and suggestions from sources too numerous to name or even recall. But I must be held responsible for the material here, not they. Readers should understand that all the examples used in these pages to illustrate communication blunders are from my own personal experiences — all were real happenings.

Finally, whatever may be the final conclusion drawn by any reader of these pages, I trust it will at least be allowed that I have sought to be meticulously Bible-based in what is said and that nothing in these pages makes the slightest suggestion that we no longer need the Holy Spirit for effective communication of the Christian faith. Quite the reverse; I submit that to study and to use divinely created mechanisms of human communication is to magnify the glory of our Triune Creator. So be it!

H.J.Appleby
Banbury 1996.

1.
Introduction

'Of the making of many books there is no end', said the wise man. Some people might feel that this is one book which need not have been written. Surely, when believers set out to tell others the truth of the gospel message, all that they need is a prayerful spirit and a strong confidence in the sovereignty of God? Why complicate the matter of communicating the Christian message by raising all sorts of 'technical' issues which apparently need to be thought about when evangelizing?

Yes, God is sovereign; if it were not so then the believer might never feel able to share the Christian message with anyone. What would be the good of inviting the occupants of a cemetery to sit up and take food, unless there was a sovereign and all-powerful God who could perform such a miracle on the dead? Make no mistake about it: the unbeliever is spiritually dead, dead, dead. Only a strong confidence in God's sovereign power can make any sense of our evangelizing unbelievers. Paul puts it well:

> I endure everything for the sake of the elect, so that they may
> also obtain the salvation that is in Christ Jesus, with eternal
> glory
>
> (2 Tim. 2:10).

The assurance that his God was sovereign kept Paul at the task of spreading the gospel message. He knew that God had an elect people who would believe when they heard that message precisely because they were the elect of God.

Yet it is this same Paul who outlines for us the basic principles of communication which we will be looking at in the following pages. Clearly he did not regard the sovereignty of God as negating the need to be aware of 'technical' matters. In this he surely challenges us if we wish to be Pauline.

But where does the Holy Spirit come in all this? Of course we need his presence and power. Nothing, but nothing can ever take the place of that. But do we need anything more? Yes! This same Spirit has given us communication guidelines throughout the Bible (which he inspired), so how can we be said to rely on him if we flout the very principles he gives?

Some say that it is revival which we really need. Wouldn't that make all our 'technical' guidelines unnecessary? There is no doubt that to live when the rushing wind of the Spirit's reviving power is abroad must be a gloriously bracing experience for believers. And at such times there is no doubt that the message of the gospel captures the hearts of multitudes of men and women with ease. The glory of God is tangible then!

At such times however, there are also extravagances; there are Satanic delusions; there are phenomena arising from the frailty of the human psyche. To read Jonathan Edwards' careful analyses of the revivals he experienced is to realize the urgent need in such circumstances for wise discernment arising from the careful understanding of biblical principles of communication. Revival brings a need for more care in these matters, not less. We have been warned by the Lord himself and by the Apostle John:

> If anyone says to you, 'Look! Here is the Messiah!' or 'There he is!' — do not believe it. For false messiahs and false prophets will appear and produce great signs and omens, to lead astray, if possible, even the elect
>
> (Matt. 24:23,24).

> Beloved, do not believe every spirit, but test the spirits to see whether they are from God; for many false prophets have gone out into the world
>
> (1 John 4:1).

How can you test anything unless you have basic principles against which to measure it! That is why the Bible brings us so many guidelines.

There have been prominent preachers and teachers much used by God who have never said a word about studying principles of communication. If they did not need to do so, why should we? The answer is that we need to do so because we are not them! Such people are raised up by God in particular times to carry out particular ministries; they are providentially equipped instinctively to follow the principles which the Scriptures so frequently illustrate. They should be models from whom we can learn. Not that we should slavishly become little clones of them but we will find, if we look carefully, that they used in their day exactly the biblical ways which we ought to be applying to communicating the Christian message in our day. In no way do such examples cancel out the need for us to study rightly to represent the Saviour to those around us; rather, they urge us on to be the best that we can be in *our* circumstances.

> Many preachers in the United Kingdom have tried to recover the Puritan emphasis on expository preaching. Some have even gone to the length of trying to preach sermons of Puritan length and with the same kind of structure, quite forgetting that what was appropriate in a defunct culture might not be nowadays ... We do not need 18th century Christians today, but modern Christians of 18th century calibre. We do not need and therefore should not pray for another Spurgeon. We must ask the Lord for gifted and consecrated preachers who will speak to our own time and culture ... We need to be alive to the danger of assuming that because God worked in certain ways in the past, we can reproduce the results by copying the approach right down to matters of detail.
>
> *(Learning from Church history:* A paper by J.P.Arthur)

This is not to say that God is under an obligation to use some of us because we have our method worked out so well. For him ever to use any of us in evangelism or to receive us in worship is an astonishing wonder. Nor are we limiting him by arguing that he will not use us when we fail to employ biblical principles. In his sovereignty he can be — and has been — pleased to use the unusual in his purposes. But none of this justifies our being careless in how we do things, or in wilfully neglecting the clear biblical principles of communication.

Unbelievers need to hear the one message of the gospel wherever and whenever they live. That need is constant. Why then, should we be so concerned about adapting the presentation of that message to different people in different times? The answer is that not to do so is to talk a foreign language. An (apocryphal?) tale is told of German missionaries in Africa who felt that the native people should be taught German in order to receive the gospel message instead of the missionaries learning the tribal tongue! It is true that all unbelievers have the same spiritual need but their perception of what they need will vary greatly according to the presuppositions of their culture. Not carefully to adapt our approach, therefore, to those perceptions will be as foolish as trying to teach by using an unknown language in an African village.

The burden of the pages which follow is that the Bible has much to say on the subject of communicating gospel truth. Just as we would not dream of carelessly ignoring the truth itself, so we cannot justify being careless and unbiblical in the way in which we present that truth to others.

Our purpose is not merely to study principles of communication but instead to argue that those principles are divinely designed and biblical. To be wilfully ignorant of what the Bible has to say on this subject would be even more foolish than stupidly to ignore the fundamental rules of Nature in some way. It would be foolish to challenge the law of gravity by leaping unprotected from a cliff-top. Is it not even more unwise to assume that God is not concerned with how he is represented to men and women? We should not ignore the guidelines he has provided. That is the justification for writing this — yet one more — book in order to look at the biblical guidelines for the communication of God's truth. Scripture is our textbook; how can we not heed its lessons?

In brief

There is biblical evidence to suggest that guidelines for communicating his truth have been given us by God. Problems arise if we do not follow them.

To think about

'The large crowd was listening to him (the Lord Jesus Christ) with delight' (Mark 12:37). Why do you think that was? Can you suggest why the general public in Britain today does not listen similarly to gospel preaching?

2.
We have problems

An open-air meeting was in progress in the shopping precinct. I watched a man as he stood there listening. He looked intelligent. I moved up to him and asked if he was interested in the Christian message. 'Oh no!', was his answer, 'It's utterly irrelevant in this day and age'. And with that, he walked away. The speaker at that open-air meeting was earnestly explaining the gospel message, but in words that were strange to anyone with no knowledge of Bible language. The listening stranger was desperately wrong, of course. Christian thinking is not utterly irrelevant today — far from it. The world flounders without it. But what he was hearing was irrelevant to him; it was a 'foreign language', only understood by those 'in the know'.

'I did enjoy the carols, but I couldn't understand what that man was on about', she said as we took her home after the special evangelistic carol service. The vital message of Christmas obviously hadn't reached her. She had enjoyed singing (uncomprehendingly) the familiar words of those carols. She knew the tunes but not the truth.

The minister was unwell and had been absent for several weeks. Other preachers had been responsible for the ministry. After a few weeks of this the minister received a letter from an eight year-old girl. 'Please come back soon', she pleaded, 'I could understand what you used to say, but I can't understand what these other men say'.

'Pastor', asked the young lady, 'What is an 'Ebenezer'? And how do I raise one?' The minister had been thanking the Lord, in his prayer, that the church on this anniversary occasion could raise another 'Ebenezer'. (There are some ministers who regularly use that sort of symbolic language). The building was a very plain nonconformist chapel; looking round one couldn't see anything that suggested an 'Ebenezer' had been raised! To his credit the minister sat with the young lady and told her the Old Testament story in which the name 'Ebenezer' is used (1 Sam. 7:12). But would it not have been better to have more simply thanked the Lord for all his help during the year, which was the significance of the 'Ebenezer' stone, rather than to cause someone to puzzle over the expression?

The train came to a halt and the door of the compartment was opened to admit an Indian gentleman who was obviously an educated Hindu. Seeing the Europeans already there and wishing to be friendly to visitors to his country, which had by then enjoyed independence from British rule for some years, he asked in well-spoken English, 'May I know who you are, please?' Instantly the missionary replied, 'We are the servants of the most High God'. Gloriously true! But silence descended upon the compartment from then on.

Clearly, the task of communicating the gospel message confronts us with problems. And these problems need to be taken seriously by Christians because the communication of the message of Christ is an inescapable obligation laid upon every Christian disciple; there is no opt-out clause. 'Go!' was the last command of the Lord Jesus to his followers (Matt. 28:19). And since that word stands until 'the end of the age', it obviously still applies. Having gone, we are under obligation 'to make disciples ... and teach them'. If no one has learned, have we taught? Can we even be said to 'have gone' anywhere if we didn't reach anyone intelligibly?

Studies in how to communicate effectively have mushroomed from the time of the Second World War. Communicating propaganda came to be regarded then as a very important weapon of war; the search for effective methods began in earnest. We shall look briefly at this search later, in Chapters 7 and 11. Since those days, the galloping development of western society with its technological advances in available media tools, its heavy dependence upon advertising, its researches into patterns of human behaviour and processes of thought, have all relentlessly and increasingly driven the search for ways of communicating effectively to change people's attitudes. The 'world' wants its disciples, too!

We are not talking here about psychiatric manipulation or 'brain

washing'. These can be ways of changing people's attitudes by first
deranging their mental processes or wrongly stirring their emotions.
That is to degrade and insult people. No Christian, believing the
biblical truth that men and women are made in the image of God,
would want to come within a million miles of that.

Nor are we concerned with marketing techniques. The society in
which we live today is developing a 'consumer mentality' under the
bewitching influences of supermarkets, shopping precincts and the
insistent persuasion of T.V. advertising. Their implied message is
that to have all they offer is really to be someone whom people will
admire. But that is not the Christian message and must not become
so. Christian communicators are concerned only to make crystal
clear that God is the Someone to whom we each have to answer.

> The Word of God is not for sale; and therefore it has no need
> of shrewd salesman. The Word of God is not seeking
> patrons; therefore it refuses price cutting and bargaining;
> therefore it has no need of middleman. The Word of God
> does not compete with other commodities which are being
> offered to men on the bargain counter of life. It does not care
> to be sold at any price.
>
> (Karl Barth, quoted in *God in the Wasteland:* David F.
> Wells)

What concerns us in these pages is how to communicate effectively,
using the God-given intelligence of the hearer and the God-given
guidelines for doing so. We are concerned to learn how to expose the
Bible message as plainly as we know how, so that nothing we say
or do will cause it to be misunderstood. We are asking, How did God
and his servants communicate in Bible times?

Christians ought to be more concerned about successful communication than anyone else. What more important message can there
be than the biblical message? The acceptance of it — or the rejection
of it — spells the difference between heaven and hell. How desperately wrong was the open-air listener who thought that the gospel
message was irrelevant. How sad that our carol service lady missed
it altogether. What a pity that the eight year old needed to complain.
What a shame that the pastor's anniversary prayer lost its value for
a young lady because he used a metaphorical allusion from another
culture that she didn't know. What a shame to have 'stunned' the

Hindu gentleman into silence by such a heavyweight reply. In each of those cases the fault was not all on the side of the listeners. In each case the speakers were not as concerned as they ought to have been about the processes of communication. We do have problems! Richard Baxter of Kidderminster had it exactly right:

> He that would be understood must speak to the capacity of his hearers.
>
> *(The Reformed Pastor:* Richard Baxter 1856)

It isn't merely that Christians have the best message and therefore ought to be its best communicators. The Christian's God is the most superb example of unsurpassed ability in communication we could ever find. That fact ought to make Christians long to be the best possible communicators in order to reflect the excellence of their God. He is a Triune Being, yet One in holy essence. The Bible shows us, in the mysterious nature of the Trinity, that what the Father knows the Son knows and what is known to Father and Son the Spirit knows. There are no secrets, no ignorances, no selfish joys in the Person of the Godhead; the Three are magnificently One. God is LIGHT! The splendour of that divine 'interpenetration' of the three Persons results in a sublime perfection of communication. There is no darkness in him at all.

There is a further incentive which should motivate Christians to be concerned to communicate effectively. Humanity is created in the divine image, we are told: 'in the image of God he created them' (Gen. 1:27). So when we fail to communicate properly we are failing to be truly human; we are insulting the image of God in us and in our hearer. Communication is the basis of human society; enemies misunderstand each other but close friends 'read' each other's minds. We are ill at ease, and a little frightened maybe, in the presence of those who by some consequence of illness or age have tragically lost the ability to express themselves or to understand what they hear. Vacant minds, blank looks, useless tongues — we instinctively know that this is an unhappy caricature of what being human really means: the image of God has been cruelly damaged. It is damaged, also, when we *are careless in communicating*.

The biblical objection to idolatry arises from the fact that God is the supreme example of communication. The wickedness of idolatry is that the idol is such a travesty of this truth. God is a

communicator and created us also to be such. Idols 'have mouths,
but do not speak; eyes, but do not see. They have ears, but do not
hear.' (Ps. 115:5). Can there be anything more opposed to the true
nature of God and therefore to the true nature of humanity? Is it any
wonder that God's wrath is declared against such a wicked perver-
sion of the truth? An idol is an affront to God's love of effective
communication.

The Bible also speaks of God's hatred of liars. The lie is a
deliberate, calculated distortion of truth — and therefore a sin
against the openness of communication as God intended it. A liar is
a child of Satan who is 'the father of lies' (John 8:44). Whether the
failure rightly to use the God-given ability of communicating is
because of ignorance, or carelessness in the matter, or because of
wilful intention to suppress the truth, all are the denial of our
responsibility to reflect the image of God in us and in our hearers.

Nor is the Christian who is concerned to communicate effectively, blazing some new unbiblical trail or adding to Scripture in
setting out to learn how best to communicate the gospel message. As
we shall see, there are so many examples of God's continual care
how he revealed himself before and during the ministry of Christ.
There is the apostolic example seen in the record of the early church.
And now we also have the advantage of the intensive research of
recent years into what makes a successful communication — the
results of which, perhaps not too surprisingly, have become steadily
more biblical as research has proceeded because it was the Christian's God who designed the human brain and its mental functions.
He obviously knows what works best for communication among his
creatures. We can learn by seeing how he, and his apostles, did it.
And the more accurately scientific discoveries trace out the process
that the Creator first fashioned, so the more consistent will be the
findings of science with biblical principles.

We will work out some of these principles in detail in later
chapters. But we begin with the problems which the Christian
communicator faces. The first is a problem unique to the Christian
situation; the secular communicator knows nothing of it. The
message of the Bible is a message which requires both mental and
spiritual comprehension in the hearer. It is not merely a matter of
mental grasp, as is secular communication. Jesus spoke of people
being unable even 'to see the kingdom of God', let alone 'to enter
it', without their being 'born anew' (John 3:3). The Christian is

faced with the task of conveying a spiritual message to non-Christians who — because of the damage that sin has done to the human personality — have only a mental ability to grasp it, if they will. Spiritually, the unbeliever is 'dead' (Eph. 2:1). This situation seems to be at an impasse. How can a mind which is closed to spiritual truth be opened?

Curiously enough this difficulty drives us again to a study of communicating principles. Not that we can, by any of our skills, cause a person to be 'born anew'. As Paul put it, we can sow the message, we can water it, but it has to be 'God that makes it grow' (1 Cor. 3:6). But as we have already seen, it is God who has designed the whole process of communication as a reflection of his nature. What more likely then that, in all normal circumstances, he should use the very principles he has designed to reach into the mind which he will graciously open to new birth?

So it is urgently necessary that Christian communicators are careful to use those divinely created pathways for the message. It is not a mark of spiritual-mindedness to be careless of any of the Creator's natural laws by which our material world functions. Indeed, in uncovering the physical laws of the universe we tread in God's footprints. It honours him to do things his way; it benefits us to do things his way; it insults him to behave indifferently to his ways. That is especially true in regard to the act of communicating.

But we do have this first problem. How do we take a spiritual message to those without the ability to perceive spiritual things?

'Those who are unspiritual do not receive the gifts of God's
Spirit, for they are foolishness to them, and they are unable
to understand them because they are spiritually discerned'
(1 Cor. 2:14).

We begin by acknowledging that there is no way, with all the skills we might muster, whereby we can produce in anyone that ability to discern what is spiritual. The faith to believe in Jesus Christ as Saviour and Lord and the attitude of repentance for sin are experiences of the new life which can only be miraculously given to a human spirit by the power of the Spirit of God himself. The Bible is perfectly clear about that (John 1:13).

Yet the Bible is equally clear that the biblical message is intimately involved in the creative act which brings to birth a spiritual capability in the human soul. Writes James, 'In fulfilment of his own purpose he gave us birth by the word of truth' (James 1:18). And Peter confirms that believers are 'born anew ... by the living and enduring word of God' (1 Peter 1:23). The presentation of the biblical message is normally the instrument by which faith and repentance (the expressions of a new spiritual life created in a soul) come to view. Could there be a stronger reason to compel us to think carefully about communicating that message? Are we to expect the Spirit to perform two miracles — one, to remedy our carelessness in presenting the message and then another, to create new spiritual life in our hearers? Dare we so belittle our responsibility to teach?

> Our zeal for persuading lost souls of their need of salvation must not be undermined by a wrong view of the Spirit's work or the order of salvation. The Holy Spirit uses our words of witness. We realise that no one will turn to God unless the Spirit works, but we must speak as though people *can* understand. (*italics mine* — HJA)
> (*Biblical strategies for witness:* Dr Peter Masters)

Of course God does not use any one of us as his messengers because we are so expert at expressing his message to our hearers. Yet it has always been one of his gracious ways that his message should be brought to men and women through his agents. The reason for that lies outside the scope of this book. But, we repeat, the consequence of that must surely be that those agents need to be concerned rightly to represent the message with accuracy, relevance and care. Can we ask God's blessing, otherwise? We must always hold in balance both our human responsibility and God's sovereignty in the affairs of his kingdom. To ignore either is to fall into error.

And perhaps we need to make the point here that it is a message which is to be communicated, not a formula of special words; communication is a matter of transferring a message by the most effective words. It is God's message in the gospel which is essential, not any specific collection of nouns, adjectives and verbs.* Paul did

---

* I did once hear it strongly argued that no one would be saved through the use of the New International Version of the Bible. I suspect the passing of time has seen that assertion made somewhat less impressive.

not use a single Bible quotation when he preached on Mars Hill —
yet the message of that sermon is thoroughly biblical throughout and
there were converts! The church in Athens lasted for centuries.

God has now given us all we need to know of his truth in the
completed Scriptures. Our responsibility is to use Scripture by
conveying its message, more than by a bare reciting of the words;
such a recital will be meaningless unless their message is understood. And since the message we actually send is what our hearers
understand by what we have said and not necessarily what we think
we have said, we come back again to the importance of taking care,
the best way we know how, to communicate efficiently. That is the
subject of the rest of this book.

In brief

The Christian believer has the highest of motives to strive to spread
the gospel message effectively. To do so requires an understanding
of those problems that can hinder the process.

To think about

'Young man, sit down, sit down. When God pleases to convert the
heathen, He'll do it without consulting you or me'. Is that biblically
true? Does the use of human means necessarily belittle the sovereignty of God — or, on the contrary, enhance it?

3.
That first problem again

The Christian communicator is continually confronted by the fact that those hearers who are unbelievers are caught in an unenviable plight. See how the apostle Paul put it — and he should know, for he had once been an unbeliever.

> Those who are unspiritual do not receive the gifts of God's Spirit, for they are foolishness to them, and they are unable to understand them
>
> (1 Cor. 2:14).

Does that not bring to a sudden stop all talk about Christians needing to learn communication skills in order to take the Christian message to non-Christians? It can't be done, some might say, for such friends are in the desperate position of being 'unable to understand'.

And as if to drive the point home, Paul adds:

> In their case the god of this world has blinded the minds of unbelievers to keep them from seeing the light of the gospel of the glory of Christ
>
> (2 Cor. 4:4).

Is not Christian outreach, then, a pointless exercise? If they are unable to understand and are blinded to keep them from seeing, whatever can be done about hearers who are so hopelessly lost?

Experience certainly supports Paul's words. How rarely do we

find people hungry to learn of Christ. The tract is crumpled and
thrown into the bin. The door is closed with a firm refusal. Many
chapels and churches display more empty woodwork than great
congregations. Clergy are more often caricatured on the media as
irrelevant wimps — or portrayed as silly, or even dangerous,
fanatics. And Christianity itself? Why everyone knows nowadays
that it is one among many faiths, any one of which is as good as any
other.

Curiously, the same apostle Paul who described the 'impossibil-
ity' of the success of Christian outreach in our unbelieving world
because it is blinded, also turned out to be a most energetic — and
successful — evangelist. And it is undeniable that the Christian
church and its message have remained — indeed, have spread
world-wide — in this inhospitable world through all the centuries
since Christ. In addition to that, every once in a while, here and there
in the world here have been splendid outbursts of spiritual power
among men and women which have produced dramatic revivals of
the awareness of the reality of Christian truth and of the very
presence of God on earth.

So, Christian communicator *(and that is the obligation of every
believer)*, how are you to understand your task in this far-from-
simple situation?

We need to sit alongside the eleven troubled men in that upper
room, where Jesus talked to his friends about what would happen
when he had gone from them. He was leaving them facing a hostile
world and yet Christ told them they were to testify on his behalf,
even though their hearers, by killing them, would think they were
pleasing God. What a prospect! But listen to Jesus' words:

> And when he (the Holy Spirit) comes, he will prove the world
> wrong about sin and righteousness and judgement
>   (John 16:8).

So it is not to be the grossly unequal contest of eleven humble men
against a hostile, unbelieving world. The Holy Spirit is to come in
a new way! It is his task to do the persuading, the convincing, the
convicting of unbelievers that Christian truth is truly truth. He will
do the proving, to the world of blind and incapable-of-understand-
ing people, that the message of God is to be attended to. What a relief
that must have been to those eleven troubled men. They were not

expected to do what is humanly impossible; the Spirit would do that. They were to do what was possible for them to do — to witness accurately, and then to rejoice at the power of the Spirit to do what they could not. What confidence that gave them, *and can give to us*. By our weakness the Spirit's strength is made plain (2 Cor. 4:7).

In part 2 of his *Introduction to the science of missions* J. H. Bavinck introduces us to the term 'elenctics' which, though not commonly used, describes something which is of first importance to us at this point. He explains the meaning of the term as follows:

> The term 'elenctic' is derived from the Greek verb *elenchein*. In Homer the verb has the meaning of 'bring to shame'. In later Attic Greek the significance of the term underwent a certain change so that the emphasis fell more upon the conviction of guilt, the demonstration of guilt. It is this latter significance that it has in the New Testament (A.V. 'convict').

Quoting a number of instances of the use of the term (Matt. 18:15; John 16:8; 1 Tim. 5:20; Jude 15; Rev. 3:19) Bavinck notes:

> From these texts it is clear that the word in the New Testament is regularly translated as rebuking, but then in the sense that it includes the conviction of sin and a call to repentance ... only the Holy Spirit can do this, even though he can and will use us as instruments in his hand. Taken in this sense, elenctics is the science that is concerned with the conviction of sin ... it is the science which unmasks all false religions as sin against God, and it calls heathendom to a knowledge of the only true God.

Jesus used this word *elenchin* of the ministry of the Holy Spirit in the world of unbelief (John 16:8 'to prove wrong'), and related it to:

a. the sin of not believing in Christ
b. to wrong views of unbelievers about what righteousness is
c. to opinions and judgements of unbelievers which are wrong

Here therefore we have identified the three areas of unbelief against which, if we testify faithfully, the Holy Spirit will be specifically supporting us:

a. There is the evidence of historical records that there was a Jesus Christ. There is the evidence of historical records that Jesus said and did things which only God could do. There is the evidence that men and women through the centuries have spoken of having an experience of the presence of Christ which has altered their lives. There is the evidence of the expanding Christian church among all nations. Refusal to accept such evidence as this is an arrogant sin; there is no need to commit murder to be a sinner. Not to believe in Christ is sin enough.

b. Talk to non-Christians about the subject of righteousness and it rapidly becomes clear that their views of what pleases God are not those of the Bible. Of his fellow countrymen the apostle Paul had to say:

> ...being ignorant of the righteousness that comes from God, and seeking to establish their own, they have not submitted to God's righteousness
>
> (Rom. 10:3).

The unbelieving world is still engaged in the task of seeking to justify itself, to create its own standards of righteousness careless of the fact that God, through his prophet Isaiah, has warned that:

> We have all become like one who is unclean (i.e. ceremonially unable to approach the presence of God in the Temple, because) ... all our righteous deeds are like a filthy cloth (i.e. a cloth soiled by menstrual discharge)
>
> (Isa. 64:6).

Emphatically, the ideas of the unbelieving world about righteousness need to be proved wrong.

c. And the judgements made by unbelievers about the truths of the Bible are plainly wrong — and always were. It was the judgement of unbelief that Christ was an impostor, and ought to be crucified. How wickedly wrong that judgement was! And every unbeliever since then who judges that Christ has nothing for him or her is standing with those crucifiers. The unbelieving world needs to be challenged as to its opinions and judgements concerning spiritual things, for those opinions are so fundamentally wrong.*

So we arrive at the question, if these are the three areas in which the Christian communicator is to focus the gospel challenge to unbelief, how is that to be done? Christian apologists have struggled with this question from the time of the first century of Christian history: they began to attack unbelief with philosophy and the logic of reason. And Christian apologists have used the same approach many times subsequently. There is real value in this approach but it is a limited value and not without its dangers:

> Apologetics, in so far as it is valid, consists of two things: clearing away the misunderstanding of the revelation and showing the weakness of alternatives to it.
>
> *(The goodness of God:* J.W.Wenham)

One can expose the inadequacy, and therefore the folly, of the ideas of unbelief. Listen to Isaiah laughing at the idolater who takes his piece of wood:

> ... part of it he takes and warms himself; he kindles a fire and bakes bread. Then he makes a god and worships it, makes it a carved image and bows down before it. Half of it he burns in the fire ... the rest of it he makes into a god ... and says 'Save me, for you are my god!'
>
> (Isa. 44:15-17).

But the use of reason to create doubt in the thinking of the unbeliever has some dangers. First, because the chief wickedness of unbelief is not its folly but its insolence and the arrogance of the insult it offers to God. Second, because someone cleverer than we are may come and offer what seems to be an equally reasoned defence of unbelief and so encourage the unbeliever. And third, the unbelievers' faculty of reason is damaged by the effect of sin upon their nature. It is not wrong to expose the folly of unbelief, but that must not be all we do. The Holy Spirit's elenctic work is concerned to:

---

* I am indebted to Professor D.A.Carson' s *Commentary on The Gospel of John* for this understanding of John 16:8.

> ... convict the world of *guilt* in regard to sin, righteousness
> and judgement
>
> (John 16:8, N.I.V.).

Elenctics is concerned not merely with the folly of unbelief but also
with the guilt of it. To repeat, unbelief is not simply an intellectual
problem: it is a moral problem. For the creatures to reject the Creator
is proudly to disown a significant relationship and to despise the
wisdom of their Maker. To confront such insubordination with
logical arguments alone allows the hearer to suppose that his or her
faulty reason is adequate to dismiss the matter. It is the conscience,
not simply the reason, which must be brought to realise that
unbelievers are already under God's wrath (John 3:36).

It may seem that we have increased intolerably our problem of
taking spiritual truth to the unspiritual now that we are concerned
with the producing of guilt and not merely with the exposing of
folly. If the logic of reason is a limited tool against unbelief, what
is there left for us to use? There are, mercifully, certain other factors
to be kept in mind.

For instance, every person is made in the image of God. True, the
image is marred as a consequence of the damage that the entry of sin
has done to the whole creation. But there remains in every human
heart at least the shadow of an idea that there is a God although that
idea will not be according to the revelation of God in Scripture.
There may be a deliberate and heavy suppression of that truth. But
the possibility — for it cannot conclusively be ruled out — that there
could be a God is realised to a greater or lesser degree by all but the
exceptional human being. This is explored more fully in Chapter 16.

> For the wrath of God is revealed from heaven against all
> ungodliness and wickedness of those who by their wicked-
> ness suppress the truth. For what can be known of God is
> plain to them, because God has shown it to them
>
> (Rom.1:18,19).

Moreover, the religious idea is world-wide; there are faiths everywhere. That must reflect the fact that human beings are basically
meant to be religious creatures. The ability to worship something —
even if it be only oneself, or another human being — is universal.
And that fact, combined with the inexhaustible grace of God, means

that there is no human being beyond the reach of the Spirit of God or who cannot be persuaded by him. The basis for the persuasion is already in place, to some extent, in the built-in human awareness that there might be a God, and in the human instinct to 'worship' something or someone.

Then again, human nature is itself a ready-made bridge between each human being and every other one. If the unbeliever is a sinner, so is the Christian; if the unbeliever needs the grace of God, so does the Christian; if the unbeliever longs for something better, so does the Christian. The Christian communicator and the listener have some common ground. The Christian can come with all the authority of personal experience to address the need of the unbeliever. It is worth considering whether by the (commendable) 'Reformed' emphasis upon expository preaching we have not lost something of the value of personal testimony. It should not be 'either-or' but 'both-and'.

The Christian communicator has the enviable advantage of being able *from personal experience* to talk about Jesus Christ and his relevance to the great questions of who God is, what worship is, and how we are to deal with the questions of our sinfulness and our hopes for something better. Since the Holy Spirit loves to glorify Christ, what better thing can the Christian do than talk about Christ and his relevance to us?

Significantly enough, when Jesus outlined the three things about which the Spirit was coming to convict the world he set them, as we have seen, in a certain order. First, the sin of unbelief; then the error of human ideas of righteousness; finally the unreliability of human judgements. To be wrong about Christ leads to wrong views about what pleases God and that mistake leads to unreliable opinions about what God says. There you have the history of every non-Christian on earth, in three brief steps!

To sum up: the first problem of bringing a message of spiritual things to the unspiritual is not without hope of solution. The Christian actually has some things in common with the unbeliever and in addition has a powerful leader — the Lord the Spirit. And while the logic of reason can do a work of demolition upon unbelief, the Christian message must be put at once in the cleared place; the Spirit loves to glorify Christ. The slave trader who became a Christian had it exactly right when he wrote:

'What think ye of Christ? is the test
To try both your state and your scheme,
You cannot be right in the rest,
Unless you think rightly of Him.'

(John Newton)

That is quaint language by today's standards. But the message of
that language is true in any age.

In brief

Unbelief is the result of a wicked blindness to spiritual things. Yet
Christian outreach is not a hopeless task, for the Christian commu-
nicator shares some common ground with every believer and the
Holy Spirit's activity in the world is precisely to give spiritual sight.

To think about

'The devil ... that proude spirite ... cannot endure to be mocked.'

(Thomas More, 1478-1535)

'The best way to drive out the devil, if he will not yield to texts of
Scripture, is to jeer and flout him, for he cannot bear scorn,'

(Martin Luther, 1483-1546)

Seen outside a Baptist church building!
'Our' means 'us inside this church building.'
'You' means 'you on the pavement outside the fence.'

4.
A second problem

The writers of the New Testament use only two adjectives when describing the gospel message: it is a 'glorious' gospel and it is an 'eternal' gospel. No other adjectives are adequate, apparently, to express the essential nature of the good news we Christians are to talk about. But in a world full of fading tinsel how does one talk effectively of something at once both 'glorious' and 'eternal'?

I quote from the late Professor John Murray:

> ... without question, communication of the gospel to a world whose patterns of thought are so alien is one the most challenging tasks confronting the Church ...
> *(Claims of Truth:* Banner of Truth)

For instance, 'grace' can be a girl's name. And in a competitive society where everyone is encouraged to live by 'their right' to this or to that without too much regard for the welfare of others, the gentle loveliness of the Bible word 'grace' is lost to common understanding. And further examples will come to mind:

'Revelation' is either a kind of suitcase or the latest piece of sleaze in the tabloid newspapers. The breathtaking wonder of the fact that 'revelation' means that the infinite God has (as Martin Luther put it) 'stooped to lisp' something of his Otherness in little syllables we can just grasp, is lost. For instance, the Volkswagen 'Golf Mark II' was advertised as the 'Born Again Golf'. Thus, the miracle of the life of God entering the soul of a human being — new birth — becomes an advertising gimmick to describe a chunk of metal doomed to age, rust and decay.

Nobody recommends 'blood' for washing in nowadays (as if they ever did!). Being 'washed in blood' has more to do with terrorism or ethnic cleansing in common parlance today than with a conscience which sings for joy that it is so 'clean'. And 'lamb' comes from New Zealand, mate ... (This is in no way to be understood as speaking in a derogatory manner of 'the precious blood of Christ, like that of a lamb without defect or blemish' (1 Peter 1:19) but simply to indicate how that truth which is so loved by and so significant for Christians can be totally misunderstood by unbelievers if unwisely used when speaking to them).

There are other words which have fallen out of our old dictionaries and, like the chameleon, now mean something that blends better with today's environment. Be careful how you call your brother 'gay'! 'Living in sin' has probably been vacuumed empty of any meaning: it used to refer to unmarried couples; we call them 'partners' now. (What has that done to the lovely word 'partners'?). A child born out of wedlock (and the number of them has hugely increased in the last decade) is now 'a love child': what has that done to the beautiful word 'love' which used to include the thoughts of enduring faithfulness and commitment?

And what is 'sin' in today's general talk (if you hear the word used at all!)? It is certainly not used of disobedience to God's Word. 'Wicked!' (with the exclamation mark) means 'superb' now; 'sad' means 'contemptible', not 'miserable'. 'Sick' means mental illness more than biliousness. 'Free gospel offer' — well, free offers are things on the sides of the cornflakes packet nowadays, with no ill consequence if you ignore them and probably only a bit of cheap plastic if you send up for them. 'Holiness' — isn't that the Pope?

'Why are you doing this?', a bystander asked at the open-air meeting. 'The Lord Jesus has told us we must preach to every creature' was the eager reply. 'Every creature?', he repeated, in some bewilderment! For him, 'creatures' meant creepy-crawly insects! And further, if it isn't enough to lose so may of the words we formerly used when we talked about the gospel, there seems to be even fewer people who want to hear the gospel, anyway! Os Guiness puts it plainly:

> I would suggest to you that if you look at most evangelism and apologetics, 90% of what we say is directed at only 10% of our contemporaries at any one moment. Brilliant though

much of it is (sic!) it does not speak to where most people are;
it assumes a high degree of interest, or openness, or need —
and yet those three things do not characterize most of our
contemporaries at any particular moment.

(from a public lecture)

On the surface, this seems to be true. No interest — no openness —
no sense of need; as far as secular, materialistic men and women are
concerned, that's a snapshot of the faces of our listeners!

Yet the message we carry declares itself to be for people who
have a need; it is for those who 'are weary and are carrying heavy
burdens' (Matt. 11:28); for those who long for light rather than
darkness; for those who are interested to 'take the water of life as a
gift' (Rev. 22:17). And, what is more, we are under solemn obligation to go to everyone with this message whether they express a
desire for it or not!

John Murray again:

> ... with all that may properly be conceived and applied in
> developing the art (i.e. of communication), how dismally we
> fail ... if we overlook the fact that in the last analysis.
> communication is dependent upon a grace we cannot com-
> mand and cannot pour into the channels of our ingenuity ... it
> is dishonour to the Spirit if we do not recognise and acknowl-
> edge our complete dependence upon his grace. But no less
> dishonouring is it when we allow our sense of dependence to
> be an excuse for sloth ...
>
> *(Claims of Truth:* Banner of Truth)

Certainly, we are driven to acknowledge our desperate need of the
convincing life-giving work of the Holy Spirit. God forgive us if, with
our use of proper communication skills we ever create the impression
that our message is merely human and not divinely glorious.

But while we acknowledge that there is this problem — human
minds are 'blinded by the god of this world' and to tear away that
curtain and let spiritual light into the soul is not within our skills —
yet, equally, there is a right process to help us bridge the distance
between ourselves and the people of the ungodly cultures which
surround us. We can, and must, communicate in such a way that

there will be at least a mental grasp of the message by our hearers. That is our task and our responsibility as witnesses, ambassadors, of the kingdom of heaven.

Having laid down the essential scriptural content of all preaching and insisted on the importance of preserving its purity, J.H.Bavinck goes on to say:

> On the other hand, it is also possible to have the best intentions and to ignore the cultural possessions of a people; to preach the gospel pure and simple, without any application to their specific characteristics. History has shown that such a procedure is also questionable ... such a method does not take seriously enough the people to whom one speaks. God, in contrast, takes us, and those to whom we speak, very seriously, and as his ministers we ought to do the same.'
>
> (*An introduction to the science of missions:* J.H.Bavinck)

Whether the message is acted upon or rejected may well be a cause of joy or sorrow to us. But if we have carefully made the message intelligible the outcome is not our responsibility. Not to exercise such care is to waste our time and energy. The apostle Paul's comment, though made initially in the context of tongues-speaking, is more widely relevant:

> ... if in a tongue you utter speech that is not intelligible, how will anyone know what is being said? You will be speaking into the air
>
> (1 Cor. 14:9).

Using words which, if we stopped to think, we would know our hearer would not understand, is to talk in 'tongues'. How can we tell the Lord that we have gone to our neighbours with his message, if all we have done is speak into the air?

Paul clearly anticipated that 'outsiders' would sometimes* come

* The implication is that this is an occasional 'accidental' happening. It does not suggest that Christian meetings must be evangelistic. The biblical thrust is that evangelism means going to outsiders rather than pulling outsiders in. If they come, well and good, provided that the worship is in plain language. But the reason for that plain language is primarily for Christian worshippers — see chapter 17.

into Christian meetings and therefore argued that what happened in those meetings should be intelligible to such people:

> Otherwise, if you say a blessing with the spirit, how can anyone in the position of an outsider say the 'Amen' to your thanksgiving, since the outsider does not know what you are saying? For you may give thanks well enough, but the other person is not built up
>
> (1 Cor. 14:16,17).

There is this problem, then, of bridging the gap between Christians and the culture of the world today. The distance between ourselves and the rapidly developing pagan culture around is growing year by year. Time was when there was at least a nominal awareness of the meaning of biblical words among men and women; there was at least a surface acknowledgement of the value of the ten commandments. True, that nominality created much deliberate hypocrisy but at the same time it allowed the usage of Christian terms with some hope of their meaning being understood, even if they were not wholeheartedly accepted.

But society has changed, is changing; the rate of change is accelerating. Which means that if we are to keep in touch with our neighbours we must know where our neighbours are culturally. We must adapt the presentation of the message to be relevant to them.

> The very point where conservative Protestantism has failed most miserably is in the realm of communication. And that failure largely has stemmed from a lack of adaptation. Behind this failure of adaptation are doctrinal and attitudinal difficulties that sometimes lead to an unwillingness to keep abreast of the times ... Paul's method of beginning with people where they are depends largely upon knowing where they are — and demands much patience.
>
> *(Studies in Preaching, Vol 2:* Jay Adams)

So what was Paul's method? He tells us clearly:

> To the Jews I became as a Jew, in order to win Jews. To those under the law I became as one under the law (though I myself am not under the law) so that I might win those under the law.

To those outside the law I became as one outside the law (though I am not free from God's law but am under Christ's law) so that I might win those outside the law. To the weak I became weak, so that I might win the weak. I have become all things to all people, that I might by all means save some. I do it all for the sake of the gospel

(1 Cor. 9:20-23).

That is the Pauline method: adaptation to the culture of those to whom he speaks. He 'makes himself a slave to all so that he might win more of them'. He 'chained himself' like a slave to the limitations of his hearers. Always and everywhere his motivation was to make the message relevant and intelligible. He did what would prosper the gospel cause in each situation; and that involved a remarkable flexibility of behaviour — even apparently contradictory behaviour.

For instance, sometimes he claimed the privileges of Roman citizenship, sometimes he ignored them; sometimes he circumcised others, sometimes he did not; sometimes he ignored Jewish ceremonial law, sometimes he obeyed it; sometimes he baptized converts, sometimes he left others to do that; sometimes he stressed his apostolic authority, sometimes he pleaded as though an inferior. None of this was ever flippant or unthinking behaviour. There is no justification for our behaving 'as the fancy takes us.'

Underneath that inspired flexibility there was no inconsistency. The one consistent basis of all his behaviour was: what, in this situation, best serves the spread of the gospel. He did not hesitate to adapt his approach 'for the gospel's sake'. We often hear talk about Pauline theology, and that is good; but, strangely, little is heard about the Pauline method.

Surely the Pauline method was God's method. When God would talk to men and women he became a Man and met and ate with them. He lived under the same Roman yoke; he wept at sorrow and sickness; he enjoyed the same joys, his feet were soiled with the same dirt of the streets and needed to be washed just like theirs. God does his communicating in an incarnational way, adapting his presentation in a 'mind-blowing' manner by coming to his hearers in their likeness (see Appendix 2):

> And the Word became flesh and lived among us, and we have
> seen his glory, the glory as of the Father's only son, full of
> grace and truth
>
> (John 1:14).

Luther got it right! See how he talks about his translation of the
Bible:

> I try to write German, not Latin or Greek couched in German.
> I try to make Moses so German that no one would think he
> was a Jew! But oh, what an immense laborious task it is to
> force the Hebrew writers to talk German. How they struggle
> against being compelled to forsake their natural manner and
> follow the crude German style! It is like trying to make a
> nightingale give up its own sweet melody and imitate the
> song of a cuckoo ... This version won't last for ever, either. In
> time, the world will need something new again and throw it
> away.
>
> (Quoted in *Luther Alive!:* Edith Simon)

Also John Calvin learned to preach in Genevan French rather than
use the Parisian French of his early years. That may seem no great
adaptation, but it made him 'at home' among Genevans and was for
'the sake of the gospel'.

It must be obvious that adaptation of the message is not without
its dangers. The message can be distorted, even lost, if the adaptation
is wrongly done. This is yet another reason why the messenger needs
to be aware of the rules of effective communication. No one
becomes a brain surgeon without a great deal of learning, careful
thought and practice. So why should we suppose that a surgeon of
souls can rush in to a situation with nothing but zeal as his or her
equipment? Think of the intensive training the disciples had in those
forty post-resurrection days.

The adaptation of the presentation is of increasing importance in
some areas of our country today because there are now communities
among us from other nationalities and of other religions. To be
meaningful in our presentation of the gospel message to them
confronts us with the necessity to understand their cultures, which
may well be a harder task than simply to address those of our own
western culture. Nevertheless we are not excused from the task

merely because of its difficulty. There are books available which can help us to approach people of other faiths*. If we have this problem we are responsible to search for answers to it.

During the eighteenth century, William Grimshaw had a remarkable ministry in Haworth and the surrounding Pennine countryside. John Newton wrote of him:

> He rather chose to deliver his sentiments in what he used to term 'market language'. And though the warmth of his heart and the rapidity of his imagination might sometimes lead him to clothe his thoughts in words which even a candid critic could not justify, yet the general effect of his plain manner was striking and impressive, suited to make the dullest understand and to fix for a time the attention of the most careless. Frequently a sentence which a delicate hearer might judge quaint or vulgar, conveyed an important truth to the ear, and fixed it in the memory for years, after the rest of the sermon and the general subject were forgotten. Judicious hearers could easily excuse some escapes of this kind and allow that, though he had a singular felicity in bringing down the great truths of the gospel to the level of the meanest capacity, he did not degrade it. The solemnity of his manner, the energy with which he spoke, the spirit of love which beamed in his eyes, were convincing proofs that he did not trifle with his people. That is the best cat which catches the most mice.
>
> (*William Grimshaw:* John Newton)

Did you notice the last few lines of that quotation? They tell us how Grimshaw could adapt so well without losing the message: 'solemnity ... energy ... spirit of love ... not trifle'. These were the factors which made it safe for him to use 'market language' as he did.

We must be aware of a danger. There can be the temptation in adaptation simply to shock or merely entertain; to dazzle the hearer with our cleverness. That thought should horrify us although at the same time we accept the rightness of adaptation. Our words must not distort the message to our hearers or we may as well not speak at all.

---

* e.g. 'To love a Muslim'; 'Telling Jews about Jesus'; both from Grace Publications.

Our presentation must be faithful to the content of the gospel; it is not our message to play with as we like. That is the second problem we have to face now — how to talk of the gospel of God with words which are correctly understood by our neighbours.

> From all my lame defeats, and oh! much more
> from all the victories that I seemed to score;
> from cleverness shot forth on Thy behalf
> at which, while angels weep, the audience laugh;
> from all my proofs of Thy divinity,
> Thou, Who wouldst give no sign, deliver me!
>
> (*Poems, 1964:* C.S.Lewis)

We move further into our study with concern and care. There is a third problem yet to be faced.

In brief

Evangelism involves human responsibility as well as divine sovereignty. We must choose our words carefully. But what are the words which will be meaningful in today's culture?

To think about

On page 42 there is a paragraph describing incidents in Paul's life when his behaviour seems to be inconsistent. Find the references and see how different behaviour in different situations served the spreading of gospel truth.

5.
Scratching where it itches

Thus far we have met two problems which confront the Christian communicator; one: the inability of unbelievers to believe spiritual things; two: our difficulty in talking their language in order to adapt our presentation of the gospel message to fit their mental grasp. Is there something else which stands between the Christian communicator and the non-Christian? Indeed, there is. Problem three: we shall not get alongside our neighbours in any incarnational way (i.e. in a way recognisable by them as belonging to their kind of person) unless we know their culture.

Paul knew how to be a Jew; he knew how to be a Gentile; but do we understand the culture of our day? Or are we still talking as if addressing the society of our forefathers? We need to explore this matter before we proceed. And here we introduce terms used to describe the social atmosphere in which we in the West live and breathe today: Modernity, and Post-modernity. We will examine these terms more fully presently.

But for now, briefly, modernity comprises those elements making up the nature of our Western culture, distinguishing it from what has gone before. The culture of today is not the culture in which the early church lived; nor is it the culture in which the great Reformation blazed; it is not the culture of the Puritan era; nor the culture of the days in which Whitfield and the Wesleys preached; nor even the culture of our grandparents' days. Today's culture is different from what has gone before. Of course, human nature is the same as always — sinful; the difference now is in the way in which that sinful nature is thinking and expressing itself to create our culture of modernity. To overlook this fact leads to scratching where it doesn't itch.

The reason why a culture creates a problem for us lies in the fact that the culture in which people live affects the way that they think. Presuppositions tend to control perceptions. If you are of the view that nothing is real or true unless you can verify it in a laboratory, then you will become a materialistic and secular person; God and religion is an unverifiable, meaningless superstition. Your scientific instruments do not detect God. Your basic thinking has shaped your conclusion about religion and will result in your fashioning a materialistic way of life, a secular culture.

Or, to take another example, this time in the area of what differing cultures regarded as a satisfying art form, let us suppose that listening to Handel's oratorio 'The Messiah' is among the most moving experiences you know. The performance often involves massed choirs, a great orchestra, the words of Scripture which seem to come alive in the music to which they are set, the triumphant 'Hallelujah' chorus. The king of England once stood up as that chorus was performed so moved was he by its magnificence and thus began the tradition which still persists of standing while that chorus is sung.

Let us suppose, however, that you wish to explain to a Tamilian in a South Indian village what a wonderful experience it is to listen to 'The Messiah'. He has never heard of George Frederic Handel. He does not know the scriptural passages. Western orchestral music is a strange noise to his ears. Will you play him a recording of it all, to try and give him the flavour of the thing?

The poor man stays baffled; what he hears is so different from what he knows as music. Accustomed to solo voices, particular ragas of notes (i.e. a melodic pattern of a small number of notes used as a basis for improvisation by Hindu classical music), complex and skilful drum rhythms — he cannot hear, in your recording, anything with which he is familiar in his understanding of music. He remains puzzled as to why you should be so moved by your 'music'. Equally, you will probably be quite bewildered by the intricate nuances of Indian classical music which bring tears of joy to his eyes!

The problem is that you both are struggling to interpret one culture from inside the 'prison' of a different culture. Now it may not matter very much whether you succeed in getting him to appreciate Handel or even whether you begin to appreciate Indian classical music. But when it is a case of the gospel message being presented to someone, the issue is very much more serious; which is why this matter of the cultural 'prisons' in which we and our hearers live is a problem which needs to be seriously considered.

If you are locked into one cultural understanding of the world around you and are confronted by another set of cultural ideas, you will try to interpret those ideas in the terms with which you are familiar in your own culture. You have no other tools to use than your own presuppositions. And that is a recipe for misunderstanding. Let us look briefly at some biblical example of this kind of misunderstanding. We will explore the matter more fully in Chapter 11.

Jesus talked to Nicodemus (John 3) about being 'born again'. Nicodemus was locked into a culture of physical religious rituals performed, it was thought, in order to please God. The phrase 'born again' presented him with a big problem. Here was a piece of physical ritual he had never heard of and he could not conceive how it could be done. Could it really be possible to enter a mother's womb and be born a second time?

Jesus talked to a woman beside a well (John 4) about 'living water'. For her 'living water' meant water bubbling up from a spring and not water merely draining through the soil and collecting in a well — 'dead' water. And the suggestion that she might have a fountain of living water all to herself was an exciting possibility. No more weary walks to the well in the heat of midday; no more buckets and ropes and pulleys!

Jesus talked to the crowds (John 6) about eating his flesh and drinking his blood after the miracle of feeding thousands with one boy's lunch of loaves and fishes. Jews drink blood? Eat human flesh? This was a ghastly concept to them. While Jesus was talking about precious spiritual experience, they were interpreting what he said as cannibalism. They shook their heads and walked way.

Keep in mind the fact that these were not irreligious people. From that point of view they might seem to have been the easiest people to talk to about spiritual things. But they were locked in the 'prison' of a formal, ceremonial religion. From inside that culture they could only interpret all religious talk in terms of physical action. Their presuppositions governed their perceptions.

That this should be so when the Son of God himself was presenting the gospel message is at least some comfort to us. If the problem of cultural barriers (as well as the barrier of sinful unbelief that we have already acknowledged) confronted the Master himself, then perhaps we are not surprised if the same should happen to his servants also. But what is so much more important here is that these examples also show us how the Lord dealt with those gross misunderstandings. He did not ignore the problem; he grappled with it — and therefore so must we. For the moment we leave that aside; it comes later in our study (see Chapters 9 and 15). We must return to the matter of modernity, the name of the culture in which we live and in which our hearers are largely 'imprisoned'.

We have already seen that there is a strong biblical warrant for expressing the gospel message in those ways best calculated to relate meaningfully to the cultural ideas of those to whom it is presented. The apostle Paul had no doubt that this was correct, the Christ-like, thing to do. We have already seen his principles: to the Jews, as a Jew; to the Gentiles, as a Gentile: to the weak, as weak: to the strong, as strong.

If you examine Paul's preaching to a Jewish audience and compare it with his preaching to a non-Jewish audience you can see him working out his principles in practice. When he talks to Jews (Acts 13:16-41, for example) he takes them, from their 'Bible', through the history of God's dealings with their forefathers; speaks of promises concerning the Messiah and of the evidences that Jesus is that Messiah. He is talking within the culture of his hearers.

When he talks to non-Jews, those without the law (the Old Testament Scriptures), he uses the 'Bible' of God's creation (Acts 17:22-31, for example). That, after all, is the 'Bible' with which Gentiles are familiar. In the light of the wonders of the natural world Paul shows the logical absurdity of thinking that lifeless, man-made idols can have any significance at all, compared with the power and wisdom of a God who created such a world as ours. And consequently if there is not repentance for their folly, there can only be the judgement of the Creator for them to look forward to. He is again talking within the culture of his hearers. And we must not miss the point that he uses his knowledge of secular Greek poetry to great effect when he speaks on Mars Hill.

If we are to be Pauline in our gospel presentations we need more than an accurate knowledge of gospel truths; we need to have some understanding of today's culture — of modernity. How has it come? What are its presuppositions? What are its consequences?

Paul's method of beginning with people where they are depends largely upon knowing where they are ... conservative Christians (unlike Paul) often have assumed too much knowledge and acceptance of Christian presuppositions on the part of the audiences.

(Studies in preaching: Vol. 2: Jay E. Adams)

Modernity means the changes in social structures and in commonly held ethical standards which have accompanied the rise of the technological society which has been developing since the mid-eighteenth century, the period known as 'The Enlightenment'. Modernity means: the ideology (the basic thinking) of today's western peoples which is characterized by such factors as individualism (each one doing his or her own thing), hedonism (pleasure is the chief end of life), reductionism (everything can be explained by the use of certain natural laws), secularism (this world is all), empiricism sometimes called positivism (knowledge is only that which can be measured, weighed, examined with the senses; and anything else is at best merely subjective personal opinion, or at worst, meaningless words). Let us go through those terms again and suggest some example of what they imply:

i.   individualism
ii. hedonism
iii. reductionism
iv. secularism
v.   empiricism

i.   individualism causes the decay of the sense of community.

ii. hedonism gives rise to a scramble (sometimes even a violent one) for physical pleasure.

iii. reductionism proposes to explain everything by applying one scientific theory — for example, the theory of evolution seeks to account for the universe, our world, us, our behaviour, the growth of our moral and religious ideas: almost everything, in fact!

iv. secularism dismisses as unimportant the influence of anything that is not material.

v. empiricism and positivism lead down the path that denies that
there are such things as ethical and religious absolutes. These are the
weeds that are seeding themselves all around us in the west today —
and blowing in the wind across the developing world, too.

This is our culture. As one American professor has recently
expressed it:

> Modernity presents an interlocking system of values that has
> invaded and settled within the psyche of every person ... it is,
> to put it in biblical terms, the worldliness of Our Time ...
> worldliness is what makes sin look normal in any age and
> righteousness seem odd. Modernity is worldliness, and it has
> concealed its values so adroitly in the abundance, the comfort
> and the wizardry of our age even those who call themselves
> the people of God seldom recognize them for what they are.
>   *(God in the Wasteland;* David F. Wells)

How has modernity come about? It is not of recent origin. The
eighteenth century saw the rise in the West of many radical philosophers and writers. Until that time:

> ... what passed in Europe for knowledge about the creation of
> the world, about man's place in the world, about nature and
> society and about man's duties and destiny was dominated by
> the Christian churches. Knowledge was continually referred
> to scriptural sources in the Bible and was transmitted through
> the religious institutions of universities, colleges, religious
> orders, schools and churches.
>   *(Formations of modernity; introduction:* Stuart Hall)

Scientific discoveries in the sixteenth and seventeenth centuries
about the nature of the universe (by Kepler, Copernicus, Galileo)
followed by the work of Sir Isaac Newton all appeared to reveal a
universe which was a superb machine functioning by fixed, natural
laws that were then being slowly understood. All this was taken, by
many philosophers, as a direct challenge to the then outmoded
concepts traditionally taught by the Church in the Middle Ages.
Empiricism began to dominate clerical traditionalism. The scientist,

not the priest, became the most important authority. Miracles seemed less believable: obviously they would disrupt the magnificent machine and be contrary to established laws. There seemed less need for God; if tradition had correctly taught what the Bible said, then plainly the Bible was now proved to be wrong. (That 'if', of course, needs to be vigorously contested.) 'God is dead', announced the philosopher Neitszch. So:

> Modernity is a historical process that began in the eighteenth century with the philosophical Enlightenment. It accelerated in the nineteenth century as industrialization took place, and increased even more rapidly in the twentieth century under the impact of advanced technology and science ... To live in modernity is to live in a world of frenetic pace, noise, over-indulgence and novelty. All of these things militate against the spiritual life, and the rays of God's kingdom can be shut out by the shrillness and carnality of modern living.
>
> *(Enemy Territory; the Christian struggle for the modern world:* A. Walker)

This has been a considerable abridgement describing the rise of modernity where much more detail could have been given. But it is enough to help us to recognize the culture into which we need to speak, to see how it has arisen, and to understand how its consequences are shaping our present society. The problem is now in focus.

It is ironic that the very visual aid — the universe — which was designed by the Creator to give us the evidence of his wisdom and power (Rom. 1:19,20) has become the basis for denying that there needs to be a God at all. There could hardly be a more vivid illustration of the perversity of the blindness of unbelieving minds which 'by their wickedness suppress the truth' (Rom. 1:18).

The ultimate end of the thinking of modernity, i.e. there are no ethical or moral absolutes, no God, and nothing except what has evolved by random chance, is that our human situation is absurd.*

---

* Albert Camus, the French thinker and writer (1913-60), felt that the silence of the universe (as he saw it) over against the human longing for meaning in life created a radical disharmony that was an absurdity.

As David Wells writes:

> The assumption among the Enlightenment's proponents that meaning and morality could be discovered simply within the bounds of natural reason and without reference to God has, even in our very secular age, become even more empty. Their naive faith in inevitable progress has been torpedoed by the brutality and the manifold frustrations of the twentieth century ... By the end of the 1960's modernity had lost its Enlightenment soul. Thus it was that post-modernity began to emerge in the 1970's ... Post-modernity is proving to be the final stages in modernity, in which, as it were, the beast, now sickened and deranged, has fallen and begun to consume its own innards.
>
> *(God in the Wasteland;* David F. Wells)

In a lecture given in June 1980, Dr Lewis Thomas describes what he calls 'the wisdom of the twentieth century':

> The universe is meaningless. We bumbled our way into the place by a series of random and senseless biological accidents. The sky is not blue: this is an optical illusion — the sky is black. You can walk on the moon if you feel like it, but there's nothing to do there except look at the earth; and when you've seen one earth you've seen them all. The animals and plants of the planet are at hostile odds with one another, each bent on elbowing any nearby neighbours off the earth. Genes, tapes of polymer are the ultimate adversaries and, by random, the only real survivors ...
>
> (Quoted in *Christianity confronts modernity*: Kenneth Kantzer)

His discomfort with this notion of absurdity drives Dr Thomas to express dissatisfaction with such an idea. (Human beings, being made in the image of God cannot, even in sinful unbelief, rest comfortably with absurdity.) That discomfort commonly drives individuals to suicide, taking drugs, being involved with the occult and with other experiences which cause the adrenaline to flow, producing some sense of purpose, even if only temporarily. Even the atheist philosophers of the Enlightenment period struggled with

the problem of explaining why their world was as it was, if there was
no God. No surprise, then, that our Dr Thomas continued:

> It is absurd to say that this place is absurd, when it contains,
> in front of our eyes, so many billions of different forms of life,
> each one in its way absolutely perfect, all linked together to
> form what would surely seem to an outsider a huge spherical
> organism ... I like this thought, even though I cannot take it
> anywhere, and I must say it embarrasses me ... We talk —
> some of us anyway — about the absurdity of the human
> situation, but we do this because we do not know how we fit
> in, or what we are for.
>
>   (ibid).

Dr Thomas is an eminent American biochemist confronted by an
intricate universe which compels him through sheer logic to illustrate the truth of Scripture: to be without God is to be without hope
(Eph. 2:12), a prospect which leaves him restless. That very restless-
ness is so often the beginning of a searching. So take heart, Christian
communicator, all is not lost to modernity! For modernity is
yielding to post-modernity — a dissatisfaction with the evident
inadequacy of modernity's explanation of the world. It is those who
are weary and carrying heavy burdens to whom the Lord himself
said, 'Come to me' (Matt. 11:28). Perhaps it could even be that this
modernity problem is not so great a problem after all. Now that we
know where post-modernity itches, we can scratch it effectively.
    Post-modernity is a help to the spread of the Christian message
in the sense that it questions the secular dogmatism of modernity; it
is more agnostic than the atheism of modernity. Modernity arrogantly asserted: there is no God but science and science will solve
all. Looking at the ruins of modernity's failures (world wars, the
holocaust, pollution, homelessness, unemployment, racism, col-
lapse of communism and fascism, economic failure, etc.), post-
modernism says: we have no confidence in your secular absolutes;
is there anything we can have confidence in? That is where the
Christian can have a foot in the door, a door which modernity
previously slammed shut.
    The question was put to Stuart Hall, Professor of Sociology for
the Open University:

It has been said that 'modern man does not reject God but sadly bids him a fond farewell'. How would you respond to that observation?

Here is the reply from Stuart Hall, printed in the Open University 'Sesame' magazine, June/July 1994:

> I think that's probably true. I don't have any personal religious beliefs, but I am not hostile to religion and the spiritual dimension of life, and as far as what has happened in the world in one sense we are irrevocably in the secular world dominated by secular and material development. In that sense God is dead, but in another sense *it is very surprising that this late in modern history, religion seems to have an enormously powerful capacity to revive.* It is probably more important in the world today, shaping what is happening, than it has been for the last 100 years, so I don't accept the easy sociological notion that we are on the inevitable path towards the secularisation of everything
>
> *(Italics are mine — HJA).*

The capacity of religion of whatever kind to revive itself is a proof that, at heart, human beings are religious creatures. That's a good place to start our communicating, even in an agnostic culture.

The pluralistic society of today with its many religions is not a final threat to the Christian communicator. Instead, pluralism is a considerable evidence of dissatisfaction of materialistic thinking, as well as being a confirmation of the religious nature of human beings. It does not so much suggest that there are many equally valid religions, as that people everywhere cannot 'live on bread alone' (Matt. 4:4). The Christian can enter such a pluralistic religious market-place meaningfully for he or she has a message of the totally adequate and relevant gospel of God.

Undoubtedly the scientific discoveries which lie behind the culture of modernity have brought many benefits in every area of daily life. None of us would be happy now to live in the pre-Enlightenment world, without all the comforts and conveniences of modernity. The criticism of modernity is not so much about its scientific advances but more concerning the agnostic assumptions those advances have spawned. As has been rightly said:

Our community is discovering, to its loss, the problems that come from rejecting a God-centred view-point. Without a moral framework, the world stumbles around not knowing what to do with the results of its astounding technology.

(The answer's not in our genes. The Briefing 153: Kirsty Birkett)

The illumination of the discoveries of the Enlightenment and since, have also cast dark shadows across the area of the welfare of human spiritual life. The era of post-modernity has dawned in which the inadequacy of scientific and secular modernity to satisfy the longings of the human spirit is being revealed. A great search for 'spiritual' experiences is taking place, however they may be brought about. Again, this provides a 'hungry' market-place in which to testify to the excellence of the gospel of God.

Nor should it be overlooked that the gospel of God is a gospel of grace, not of human endeavour. It is therefore superbly applicable to those who are disillusioned by human endeavour. It is a gospel that brings a new and divine source of energy to replace the failed resources of weary humankind. The grace of God can bring hope to the agnostic who is unable to trust sterile human thinking precisely because it is so foreign to human thinking. So the Christian communicator who presents a distinctive message of a gospel of grace has a valid entrance into today's, and any day's, confusion of thought. The one thing we must not do is to try and compromise the biblical message with secular philosophy to produce a gospel said to be more palatable to our unbelieving world. As someone has said, He who marries the spirit of this age will be a widower in the next.

We look at this matter of confronting the challenge of today's culture in more detail in chapter 16.

In brief

The Middle Ages produced superstition and empty religious tradition.
The Enlightenment produced scientific rebuttal of traditional religion.
Science produced modernity.
Failure of modernity is producing post-modern uncertainty.
Post-modernity cries out for certainties, which the Christian can supply.

To think about

Words never exist in a vacuum. They always occur in various contexts, which can often modify their meaning. Find some examples of this.

The GOSPEL

The Gospel The Gospel The

* the gospel *

....the gospel......

THE GOSPEL

THE GOSPEL

The transposition into various styles of lettering has produced different messages - different 'atmospheres' altogether!

6.
On your marks ... get set

Communication is more than the use of words. It is words *in their total context:* who is speaking? in what circumstances? how are they speaking? to whom? why are they speaking? Communication is a matter of sharing whole messages; messages are more than strings of mere words. Messages may not even use words at all. We need to explore the implication of this.

Babies communicate before they know what words are. Dogs and cats communicate — watch their tails! Clocks and traffic lights communicate. Body language communicates — the clenched fist, the scowl, the pout, the smirk, the smile, the laugh, the wrinkled brow, the kiss, corpses in coffins — these all convey messages in their contexts, *without* words. The Psalmist said:

> The heavens are telling the glory of God; and the firmament proclaims his handiwork. Day to day pours forth speech, and night to night declares knowledge. There is no speech, nor are there words; their voice is not heard; yet their voice goes out through all the earth, and their words to the end of the world (Ps. 19:1-4).

Messages without words can be misunderstood, especially if 'read' out of context. Tails that wag from side to side do not mean in a cat what they mean in a dog. A baby's cry may mean hunger, a dirty nappy, or just wind pain. Flashed headlights mean to the Indian motorist, 'Clear the road, I'm coming through'; but to the English motorist they say, 'I'll wait; you come'. Nevertheless messages can be communicated without words even if they are sometimes liable to be misunderstood.

And sometimes messages are quite different from the first and obvious meaning of their words. Again, knowing the context is the secret of right understanding. Consider the following:

> I hear someone splashing in his bath and singing happily, 'Early one morning just as the sun was rising I heard a maiden singing in the valley down below ...' I do not register the information that my friend actually heard a girl singing in the valley in the early morning. I register the fact that he feels happy.
>
> *(Teach yourself communicating:* Colin Mares)

The message sent can even be the opposite of the plain meaning of the words used. We call that sarcasm or irony. The apostle Paul wrote to rebuke the self-opinionated members of the church at Corinth as follows:

> Already you have all you want! Already you have become rich! Quite apart from us you have become kings!
>
> (1 Cor. 4:8).

Paul's message was, in fact, the opposite of those words. He was using irony. He later wrote of those same believers as being 'infants in Christ', not rich kings at all.

Clearly, then, the communicator needs to be concerned about much more than the use of the right words. Words are only part of the story; their sense may be clarified by actions but actions may either reinforce, or conflict with, the sense of the words. The context of any words can actually affect the meaning and the weight of those words. We have seen before that there needs to be an incarnational aspect to a communication to ensure its right interpretation. Think of Paul again: to Jews as if a Jew; to Gentiles as if a Gentile.

You will find chips in a fried fish shop; they have them on golf courses too; and in a carpenter's shop; a painter may well be annoyed by them; an electronic engineer will be pleased with them;

they are to be found in casinos. This shows that the differing contexts give different meanings to the same word.

God has always been very careful about the contexts in which he caused the words of his revelation to be spoken or written. That is why the inspiration of the original words of Scripture is such an important doctrine. By his inspiring (better, 'breathing out') the exact words of the revelation in precise historical, geographical, cultural and personal contexts, God 'locked' to his words the specific message that he intended. Scripture means what it meant *there and at that time.* We misconstrue it if we neglect that divine ring-fencing.

Message equals words plus total context; each of these factors can affect the others and so effect the total message. A gospel tract poorly printed and with tiny margins ('Good stewardship of space, brother!') on cheap newsprint paper says more than its words: it says its message is cheap and temporary. A chapel building fronted by a neglected garden is saying that Christians are so heavenly minded as to be of no earthly use (which is about as false an impression of the Christian faith that you could give; to be of no earthly use is a denial of heavenly mindedness. Was Christ no use on earth?). Celebration of the Lord's supper as a brief meeting after the conclusion of the main meeting could suggest it is of lesser importance. A church membership which is known in the locality for its internal quarrels ... you can finish that sentence and think of more examples.

On the other hand, the witness of believers who have earned local respect by what is perceived to be a loving, caring, clean and spiritual way of life carries far more weight than the nominal value of the words they use. The example of a consistent believer who has been exposed to observation at close quarters by a friend for a length of time is a context in which few words may be needed at all. The message is incarnate. Contexts colour words and create messages, either winsome or repelling.

Philip wanted to see the Father (John 14:8-11). He hadn't grasped the message which Jesus had been teaching. He wondered if this Jesus could be the Messiah who would reveal the Father? Jesus urged Philip to interpret the words he had heard from his Master in the light of the context of his Master's life. He would then get the message right; he would know Christ *was* the Messiah.

Thomas was struggling to believe that Jesus had risen from the dead (John 20:24-28). If you find it difficult to believe that I am Jesus who has come alive again, said the Lord, then look at the evidence that it is I — my pierced hands and feet, my torn side. In other words, read the message of my resurrection in the context of the evidence, Thomas.

The apostle Paul more than once in his ministry appealed to his lifestyle as giving validity to his words. For example:

... you know what kind of persons we proved to be among you for your sake

(1 Thess. 1:5).

This matter of contexts affecting the message of the words becomes very important when it is a matter of marrying music to words. If you intone a weather forecast, or sing the Highway code to a Gregorian chant tune, the effect is hilarious. Neither are in themselves funny: it is the inappropriate music which has changed the overall message. The tune which is set to the words 'Onward, Christian soldiers' is in marching time, reinforcing the thought of the words. The whole question of gospel pop music, rap, rock or beat, needs to be answered consistently with this principle — contexts can alter, or reinforce, messages. In Chapter 18 we look at the subject of music in more detail; for now we can state the principle: an inappropriate context can destroy a serious message; a message in a right context can be twice as powerful.

The originators of rock music had no doubts about its message; they freely acknowledged that it was an expression of rebellion against their seniors, a message of anger and even of violence set in the context of 'the permissive years' of the early sixties. One has to ask, therefore, if that can possibly be a suitable medium for the expression of the gospel words of gentleness, love, reconciliation and peace. What is the incarnated message if you combine contra-dictory components? 'The medium is the message' said Marshall McLuhan, with some justification.

Related to this matter of the importance of the contexts in which words occur is the fact that words only mean what they are used to mean. If you want to know what a word means, listen to how it is used. Languages are often living things: they develop, give old words new meanings, create new words, adopt words from other languages. Which results in the situation that the meaning of a word can be more in its use than in the dictionary definition; dictionaries commonly follow popular usage.

Dr. Samuel Johnson in the Preface to his famous dictionary (1755) wisely comments:

> The original sense of words is often driven out of use by their metaphorical acceptions — words must be sought where they are used.
>
>   *(Dictionary of the English Language:* Dr.S.Johnson)

A more recent comment (1960) confirms the good Doctor's wisdom:

> The meaning of a word is not ultimately determined by antecendent, parallel or derived instances, but by its situation in its own context.
>
>   *(The social pattern of Christian groups in 1st century:*
>   Prof. Edwin Judge)

Even when a word is originally used according to its derivation, later years may alter its sense:

> Mankind was dear bought
> by the piteous death of dear Jesus:
> he had his remedy
> by his glorious passion, that blessed lavatory.
>   *('Mankind', from 3 late medieval morality plays:*
>   A.C.Lester, Ed.)

Lavatory? Yes, originally it meant 'a place of washing'. Christians will understand how that could have described the Lord Jesus Christ and his cross. But not to be used today, definitely not.

There is also the use of religious jargon, a kind of technical shorthand, by Christians. That language may be useful to believers. For them the 'code-words' may succinctly convey a precious content. But for anyone outside the circle of believers such language will either be unintelligible or be misunderstood. Our religious culture is an unfamiliar context to those without religion and the use of such language robs them of any possibility of hearing the right message, 'since the outsider does not know what you are saying' (1 Cor. 14:16).

For example, to be 'justified' means one thing to our non-Christian neighbours, especially if they are printers by trade, but it means something quite wonderful to Christians. 'Sin' means one thing to the believer, quite another to the non-believer. And if the 'outsider' gets inside far enough to pick up a Christian hymnbook and there meets 'a thousand sacred sweets, the panoply of God, ineffable love, each in his office wait, Zion's city, bruised and broken by the fall, rebellious worms, thickest films of vice, the eyeballs of the blind', etc., what will he or she make of us singing these phrases so enthusiastically?

Perhaps it is not entirely out of place to comment that, even to the initiated, such jargon can lose its rich content through the familiarity of repetitive use. Certainly, Christian 'code-words' must be banned from gospel outreach; perhaps we even use them too much among believers. It can be very refreshing to listen to a sermon from someone who is not a trained theologian.

None of this is to suggest that God in his sovereign way cannot, will not, so work that even jargon language or a simple passage quoted from Scripture can be suddenly, unexpectedly, meaningful to the most unlikely hearer. That is an evidence of his glory! But what we are concerned with here is *our responsibility;* the Bible gives us plenty of reason to consider just that. To use the truth of God's sovereignty as an excuse for neglecting our responsibilities is heresy.

So we come back to this: what our hearers *understand*, not what we actually say, is important in any communication. The context must be right and the words must be employed in their common usage. Again, we rejoice in the truth of the full and verbal inspiration of Scripture; it guarantees what meaning we are to deduce, since God carefully placed his revelation in precise contexts so that his truth was expressed in words as they were used in that place and at that time.

This is a reason which justifies the use of modern (and reliable) translations of the Bible. Some years ago one Bible Society published a booklet listing about 600 words used in the King James Authorised Version which are 'no longer in everyday use, or now used with a different meaning.' One has to conclude that in those instances God's message in that version is no longer in words as they are used today. Which is something very different from what God did with such care when he first gave the message.

This matter of the contexts within which our words will be interpreted does mean that certain kinds of gospel outreach are more difficult than others. Knocking on a door to present God's truth to whoever comes is not an easy way to communicate. Some knowledge of the neighbourhood, that state of the paint-work on the door, the look of the garden — these are all factors to be sensitively noted. Prior publicity in the area can help as an introduction. And it is even better if the neighbourhood is already aware of a loving concern for them by the local Christian community.

Outreach by means of radio — hospital, community, missionary — is another hard task. It may be very difficult to be aware of the contexts in which our words will be heard. When the matter of broadcasting a religious service over the B.B.C. was first mooted in the early days of broadcasting, considerable doubt was expressed as to the wisdom of such an act. The broadcast might be heard by gentlemen in public houses with their hats on! That is not quite the problem today. Nevertheless there is still a problem, for radio can reach into many varied situations and contexts about which the speaker needs to find out. (See Appendix 5).

Even a Christian tract, *distributed indiscriminately,* comes up against the same disadvantage: what sort of person will receive it? It is not like a book which readers can choose to have, or not, after examining it, should they so wish. The tract is thrust into people's hands. However, if it is concerned with some matter which is widely known and topical at that time, or concerns various special days such as Easter and Christmas, it has some advantage. But even so it must speak the language of the 'common man' who has no Bible. Whether or not a simple tract can say enough of the gospel message to make sense to people wholly ignorant of biblical concepts is yet another problem to be faced today.

There is no suggestion that these methods should not be used because they are so hard. But for this reason they must be done sensitively and thoughtfully. Prayerful concern to follow biblical principles, as we have already seen, is to be the atmosphere in which these things are to be accomplished. There are plenty of testimonies which tell of occasions where God has been pleased to give dramatic and unexpected result through the use of, to us, hard methods. And even if he does not, assuming *we have evangelized in the biblical way*, those who received the message are without excuse and our responsibility is discharged.

This could be a good point at which to notice the fact that very often God chose to use the posing of questions as the way to communicate in hard situations. When God came to Adam and Eve (Genesis 3) he came with a series of questions — not, we observe, initially with condemnatory accusations: but, Where are you? Who told you that you were naked? Have you eaten of the tree? What is this that you have done?

Similarly, when the children of Israel were being led into the Promised Land, God instructed that certain things were to be done, in order that:

> When your children ask in time to come, 'What do these stones mean to you?' then you shall tell them ...
>
> (Josh. 4:6).

When the LORD answered Job out of the whirlwind (Chapters 38 to 41) it was by a 'whirlwind' of questions. And repeatedly in his ministry the Lord Jesus posed questions to the disciples and to others.

Questions have the advantage that in hard situations they may compel hearers at least to stop and think — even about something that, in their view, may not be immediately relevant. Questions can create doubt about preconceptions. Questions can stimulate curiosity where there is ignorance. Perhaps the Christian communicator ought to give a lot of attention to the asking of questions, especially in hard situations.

Yet the presentation of the gospel message is not limited to facing these hard situations by questions. Both secular science and biblical example point to something more and it is to this we must now turn.

In brief

Message = contemporary words plus their contexts; God was careful where and how he spoke his words. This is a biblical principle. Interestingly, scientific research agrees.

To think about

How can those who may meet the Christian faith for the first time at our hands be best protected from evangelical jargon. Can the message be shared without such jargon? Try it!

THEORIES OF COMMUNICATION

THE BULLET THEORY

THE CATEGORY THEORY

THE RELATIONSHIP THEORY

Used by kind permission of 'Cork'

7.
I love you

Chapters 8 and 9 will give a survey of how God communicated his truth to men and women throughout the years of Bible history. That survey reveals clear divine principles according to which God has always been pleased to work. These must surely set the pattern for us to follow whenever we set out to proclaim the Christian message. What is of some significance, however, is that the findings of scientific research into the communication process have arrived at similar principles. In this chapter we trace, briefly, the journey by which scientific experiment has arrived at what we shall see to be biblical principles.

Because human beings have always communicated with each other, one might be forgiven for supposing that we know by now how communication works. In fact, what we know now is that the process is intensely complex, which it was not always thought to be. The war of 1939-1945 stimulated increasing research into the subject. Propaganda was being recognized as a new and useful weapon of war. It became important to find out how to communicate one's propaganda most effectively.

Communication is a social process; it is people who communicate with each other. But people vary in character, background, age, experience, education, class, religious belief and in other ways too. The early ideas of how communication works were quickly perceived to be inadequate. It had been supposed that people were sitting targets, passively receiving any information that was shot at them: say it often enough, and loudly enough, and they will be persuaded! That was referred to as the 'Bullet theory'. But far too often those who were being hit with bullets of information refused to fall over. Audiences were clearly not to be thought of as groups of defenceless clones. The phrase 'The obstinate audience' was coined by an American psychologist to express his frustration at the inadequacy of the 'Bullet theory'.

Experiments actually began to show that communication which took the form of a stream of bullets fired repeatedly and loudly not only failed to persuade but often produced the reverse effect - a growing belligerence and resistance to what was being said. (Are we not familiar with what is sometimes called 'gospel hardening'?) Many political party broadcasts on radio or T.V. serve only to confirm sympathetic listeners in their existing views, rather than to convert listeners from one political alignment to another. Human minds have a skilful selection mechanism which scans information being received, choosing what they will receive according to what they wish to make of it. In any democratic situation audiences are active, not passive; free, not captive.

By the middle of the 1950's a 'Category Theory' was being developed in order better to explain how communication works. This theory took into account the differences among people and required an approach by the communicator which took note of the category of person being addressed. People of any one type or group, it was argued, would all respond identically to what was expected to be normal for that group. Identify your group, adapt your communication to the norms of that group, then 'Bingo!' — you have communicated. So you advertise your Rolls Royce for sale in 'The Times' or 'The Daily Telegraph' and not in 'The Sun' or 'The Star'. Yet even this theory had too many exceptions to be reliable.

It began to look as if the 'mass media' were not really so 'mass effective' after all. Communication was evidently a buyer's market. Mass media could provide the *means* for persuasion and change but were not the cause of it. Audiences are composed of people of differing types and are not to be thought of en masse, or even in watertight categories. Evidently some people had an irritating habit of acting, and reacting, contrary to the norm expected for their group. People could be affected by influences from outside their group instead of conforming to the expected norms of their group. The 'Category Theory' was still too simple to be an adequate explanation of what makes a communication successful. Even in a tightly controlled, undemocratic situation there are always some individuals who do not submit to the norm for their 'category'.

So thinking moved to a third position which might be called the 'Relationship Theory'. Instead of regarding a communication as something put *into* people, it is to be thought of as information that is shared *between* people. The closer the relationship between the communicator and the receptor the more likely it is that the process will be successful. Enemies misunderstand each other so easily; to an observer it sometimes seems incredible just how much a lack of trust between two people can distort the messages which pass between them. Long-time sweethearts, on the other hand, can often 'read' the mind of their partner almost before words are spoken. A relationship which creates trust is the highway for successful communication.

There are different kinds of relationships within which communication commonly takes place in our human experience. And in each of these relationships certain things are required to be true, both for the communicator and the receptor, if the communication is to be a success. Each of these relationships must be built on a basis of trust.

For example, first, there is a relationship for instruction and the imparting of information. In this situation the teacher is expected to give useful information which proves to be accurate and true: *the teacher must be credible.* The student must be able to see the use of what is taught and have a willingness to learn: *the student must be teachable.*

Second, there is a relationship designed to bring about some change by persuasion. Here the 'salesman' needs to have a good grasp of the receptors' environment (including their culture) in order to be able to demonstrate the need for them to receive what he has to offer. *He has to be confident of his product.* The receptors have to be willing to hear the arguments for change and see the long-term benefit which would accrue to them. They need *to realise their loss if they refuse what is being presented.*

Incidentally, the likelihood of any change being brought about in this relationship can be estimated by the following formula:

Likelihood of change =

(perceived reward) minus *(perceived loss)* divided by:
(perceived expenditure of effort)
(Nature of communication between humans: Wilbur Schramm)

Therefore, if the amount of loss for not changing exceeds the amount of reward for making the change and the effort required to make the change is not too great, then change is likely to occur. That might be an interesting formula against which to test the sermon, the Sunday School lesson or the open-air talk.

Third, there is an entertainment relationship. In this case the communicator is expected to bring about a sense of enjoyment and sometimes to stimulate the quest for further knowledge. The 'entertainer' is expected *to be a skilled performer.* The receptor may be required to 'suspend' disbelief, temporarily regarding the entertainment as reality and not fictional (in the case of drama, for example) and to respond *by an immediate emotional feeling of satisfaction.*

In all these communication relationships there must be some mutual respect between the communicator and the receptor. An atmosphere of disrespect for whatever reason will distort the message or cause the hearer's mental selection mechanism to reject what is being heard. There must be an element of trust always present. And if the situation is one in which trust can grow into deep appreciation, then that closeness makes misunderstanding or outright rejection of the communication even less likely. We shall be returning to the importance of relationship for communication success in more detail in Chapter 11.

For the Christian communicator, something of each of these 'Relationship Contracts' ought to be present in any presentation of the gospel message. The credibility of the messenger, the reward of receiving the message and the possibility of a sense of joy from the message, are all essential ingredients necessary to the communication of the gospel. Disrespect, or hostility of any degree, blocks a favourable reception of the communication. Peter isn't likely to get the right message over to Malchus after chopping off his ear! Nor is Malchus' relative very keen to hear Peter expound the gospel message, after watching him 'communicate' with Malchus (John 18:10; 18:26).

But if our Christian communicator goes to someone who is ignorant of the gospel and sees no immediate need to hear its message, how is the relationship to be established in which the message can be placed? Gospel bullets fired vigorously or even the subtlest right-for-this-category-of-person message can both fail, as we have seen. The vital context for the message must be an attitude of trust which has grown from a sense of Christian love between communicator and receptor.

That context of loving understanding will be a means of informing the communicator of the needs of the receptor and will cultivate in the receptor a sense of respect for the communicator. Thus a bridge is built across which the message can travel. But even apart from that practical point, the gospel message is surely about a God who is described as possessing a nature of holy love. How can anyone represent him adequately if there is no evidence of love?

It was a wild and stormy night as the time for evening worship drew near. The chapel building was open, lit, warm and inviting in the darkness. It was also empty. A lady approached the door a little uncertainly. 'I wonder if I might worship here', she said. 'I don't want to go all the way to my usual church tonight'. She moved down the aisle and selected for herself one of the many empty seats. After a little while another lady, obviously a 'regular' came in, moved down the same aisle and stood beside the visitor. 'You're sitting in my seat', she said, in a tone of voice which was crisp with offence. Those five words shattered, probably for good, the very possibility of bridge-building between them.

This need for a context of Christian love brings with it the need to have some regular contact with those whom we would reach with the gospel. The fact is that we are more likely to be able to put the gospel message into the context of people with whom we regularly mix than to complete strangers. Our Lord himself had more 'success' with those few men and women who were with him continuously than with the many whom he met and healed in brief contacts.

This is not to suggest that God never uses the briefest of contacts to reach out with his grace to those who may be strangers to us. Especially in times of spiritual revival even the casual contact between Christian and unbeliever has been fruitful. Those are God's special sovereign moments; we long for them. But meanwhile there is the matter of our responsibility: the need to build bridges of Christian love so that by all the means we can devise some might be saved.

We look for our audience, then, among those who are around us, in regular contact with us: relations, colleagues, neighbours, workmates, schoolmates, fellow students. Not that there is anything automatic about the process of gospel persuasion even in such circumstances. But those are the places where God has providentially placed us; the places where we may best understand those to whom we go, most easily earn their respect, and most efficiently express the message in ways tailored to their situation. We shall not then be reduced to firing off indiscriminate bullets or of wrongly estimating our listener's character. We can instead construct a bridge of Christian love which is 'made to measure', a much more winsome thing.

We turn now to consider biblical examples of God revealing his truth to men and women. He spoke in ways which revealed that he knew their circumstances intimately; he shaped his speaking to fit like a glove in their situations. He built relationships within which he spoke. He is to be our example.

Do not overlook the great wonder of this. As Creator, God surely could have burst into the consciousness of his creatures and swept them into his way of thinking by some overwhelming interference with their mental processes. But this he has not done. Can it be true that even the great Creator will not trample on the process of communication among humans with which he himself endowed them? And since he has been so careful, how can we not be the same? Let us take some time to watch God communicating in love. Biblical communication is not a matter of callous manipulation or crafty marketing; it is a matter of lovingly and humbly sharing that truth which _both_ communicator and receptor urgently need.

In brief

Bullets? No! Categories? No! Relationship? Yes! For that is how God communicates.

To think about

In what ways can _you_ foster a sense of trust between yourself and those with whom you would like to share the Christian faith?

8.
God at work

As the writer to the Hebrews puts it:

> Long ago God spoke to our ancestors in many and various
> ways by the prophets, but in these last days he has spoken to
> us by the Son. (Literally, 'in Son', perhaps suggesting the idea
> of 'in Son language'?)
>
> (Heb.1:1,2).

If we are looking for principles of communication which are biblical
we cannot do better than study the records of how God has given us
his messages throughout the years of Bible history.

How God spoke to his glorious creatures, the first man and
woman, in the garden of Eden is hidden from us. In a unique way
they three conversed together as they walked in the garden at the
time of the evening breeze (Gen. 3:8). Perhaps it would not help us
much if we did know exactly how that happened, for Adam and Eve
were gloriously sinless. After their rebellion there would always be
a space between God and those to whom he would communicate;
even Moses, to whom God spoke intimately, was not permitted
Edenic closeness. The most he was permitted to see was the
'afterglow' of the glory of God on the rocks when God had passed
by (Exod. 33:23).

We will look now at some examples of God revealing his truth,
and learn some principles from Bible history. First, we watch God
communicating with Adam and Eve after they had sinned by eating
the forbidden fruit. The serpent is cursed; the woman is punished

and Adam is punished through a curse upon the fruitfulness of the soil. Yet all is not lost; there is included the promise of a future Saviour who will put right what has gone wrong in the garden of Eden. That promise is expressed, not in terms that literally described the coming and dying of Jesus Christ, but in terms of a snake's head, a person's heel, and the way in which the one can be crushed by the other (Gen. 3:15): language which would have had a vivid meaning there and then, but conveying a message which would not become clear in literal detail for centuries! God spoke within the limits of their understanding, that is the point.

God revealed the terms of a covenant to Abram. On one occasion, Abram collected together certain animals, cut them in half and then arranged each half over against the other. There followed a scene which seems strange to us:

> When the sun had gone down and it was dark, a smoking firepot and a flaming torch passed between these pieces. On that day the LORD made a covenant with Abram.
>
> (Gen. 15:17).

As we read those words we see the grace and love of God as he humbled himself to make a covenant with Abram in the manner of those days. The making of a covenant in Abram's day was by cutting some animals in half so that the covenanting parties could walk between the halves, thus implying that if either broke that covenant they would deserve the same fate as the beasts.

Archaeology has uncovered a form of treaty used in Abram's day between the rulers of two nations which involved them slaughtering an animal and declaring their mutual confirmation of the treaty by walking between the animal pieces, thus implying a self-maledictory oath if either broke the treaty. (See, for example, *The structure of Biblical Authority*: Meredith G. Kilne).

Genesis 15 fits into the context of its day. God used the contemporary method of making a covenant. The 'smoking firepot and the flaming torch' were both implements which would be in common use by any nomad of the time. That they alone (as symbols of the presence of God) passed between the animal pieces, while Abram did not, modifies contemporary practice only to show that God's covenant with Abram was one of grace on God's part and not one negotiated with him by Abram as if between equals. God alone took the oath that he would die rather than break the covenant.

We find another example when we look at the time when Moses was keeping the flock of his father-in-law in the wilderness and God had a message for him which came through the form of a burning bush (Exodus 3:1-3). Not an unusual sight, perhaps, in such surroundings. God spoke in context. And it seems that Moses was not so much startled at seeing a bush burning but rather by the fact that the bush was not consumed. So the new message came through the familiar form of a scrubby little desert bush on fire.

Moving on to the time when God sought to deal with Pharaoh, in order that the children of Israel should be released, we discover that each of the ten plague-messages was in fact an assault on some Egyptian deity. God spoke in the language of Egyptian religion, as follows:

> The Nile was considered sacred by the Egyptians ... One of the greatest gods revered in Egypt was the god Osiris ... the Egyptians believed that the river Nile was his bloodstream. In the light of this expression it is appropriate indeed that the Lord should turn the Nile into blood! It is said that the river stank, and the Egyptians were not able to use its water. That statement is especially significant in the light of the expressions which occur in the (ancient) *Hymn to the Nile*: 'The bringer of food, rich in provisions, creator of all good, lord of majesty, sweet of fragrance'.
>
> (*Moses and the gods of Egypt*: John J. Davis).

In a similar way it can be shown that each of the other plagues confronts things which were held sacred in Egyptian religion.

> The sacredness and significance of the frog to the Egyptian is demonstrated by the discovery of amulets in the form of frogs ... The frog, to a large degree represented fruitfulness, blessing and the assurance of a harvest ... The Egyptians deified the frog and made the theophany of the goddess Heqt a frog ... One can only imagine the frustration brought by such a multiplication of these creatures.
>
> (ibid.)

The plague of gnats (mosquitoes? Exodus 8:16) was an assault upon the priesthood of the land who were noted for their physical purity and lack of any blemish. The god Uatchit was reckoned to appear as a fly. Domestic animals, such as bulls and cows, were considered sacred; there was a cow goddess, Hathor. Sekhmet, a lionheaded goddess, was supposed to protect from disease and sores. Nut was the sky goddess — presumed to defend the land from storm. But no god was able to preserve their crops from the ravages of the plague of locusts. Where was the sun god Re when such darkness fell across the land that it could be felt? How could they sing the following hymn to him now?

> Hail to thee, beautiful Re of every day, who rises at dawn without ceasing ... Thou who hast constructed thyself, thou didst fashion thy body, a shaper who was not shaped, unique in his nature, passing eternity, the distant one ...
>
> (*The hymn to the sun from El-Amarna:* Adolf Erman)

Another very important sun god was Horus, often symbolised by a winged sun disc but he was shown to be as powerless as Re.

And finally there was the great assault on the god-king himself; Pharaoh would lose his firstborn son. When God spoke, all the gods of Egypt fell silent. What God had to say was couched in terms which Pharaoh would certainly have understood, even if his wicked will resisted the message.

We move on to the giving of the law to the children of Israel who were gathered at the foot of Sinai. Moses recalls the event:

> At that time the LORD said to me, 'Carve out two tablets of stone ... and come up to me on the mountain, and make an ark of wood. I will write on the tablets the words that were on the former tablets, which you smashed, and you shall put them in the ark
>
> (Deut. 10:1,2).

Why two tablets? Was it to allow five commandments to be written on each? Was it intended that there should be some distinction indicated between duty toward God (the first tablet) and duty toward others (the second tablet)? But that obscures the fact that the two duties are inseparable. Far better to understand the necessity for two tablets in the light of the contemporary practice of that age when a covenant was made between two parties. The ten commandments were not just ten laws, they were the terms of a covenant between

Jehovah and his people, couched in the familiar covenant style of those days. A typical example from ancient times begins:

> The treaty of Mursilis with his vassal Duppi-Teshub of Amurru begins: These are the words of the Sun Mursilis, the great king of the Hatti land, the valiant, the favourite of the Storm god ...
>
> (*Quoted in The Structure of Biblical authority:* Meredith G. Kline)

Such treaties always began with a Prologue (as above) and then proceeded in an 'I-thou' style outlining the terms of the treaty. The structure of the 'ten words' follows the pattern of that day and age. Such treaties would have been sealed with a ceremonial meal, as was the case with the Sinai covenant (Exod. 24:9-11). There are other references to coventantal meals such as Gen. 26:28-30; 31:51-54; Ps. 23:5,6, and, of course, Matt. 26:26-28, the covenantal meal of the new covenant.

Each party to a treaty would have a copy to keep as a reminder of their responsibilities, so two tablets were required. The two tablets of the Israelites were both deposited in the ark of the covenant in order that the copy of the 'ten words' was kept *both* in the middle of the camp of Israel (Israel's copy) and in the immediate presence of the God of the covenant (God's copy), whose glory burned above the ark. Again we see that God spoke to his people in the manner of ancient practice.

Later, Joshua and the army of Israel had miraculously crossed the Jordan (though it was in flood) and were camped by Jericho. This was the first time they had ever encountered a walled city and it had been the fortified cities that had most frightened the spies whom Moses had sent to report on the land. So this is a moment when God chose to speak to his servant Joshua.

> Once, when Joshua was by Jericho he looked up and saw a man standing before him with a drawn sword in his hand
> (Josh. 5:13).

God spoke to a soldier by appearing as a soldier; it was a meeting between two commanders (v.14).

Again, Jeremiah prophesying from Judah is concerned for the

welfare of his fellow-countrymen who had been taken captive to Babylon. He urges them not to forsake Jehovah their God though they now lived in a land where false gods were worshipped. In the middle of a long Hebrew poem on the glory of the LORD who is the true God, Jeremiah suddenly says:

> Thus shall you say to them (the Babylonians): The gods who did not make the heavens and the earth shall perish from the earth, and from under the heavens
>
> (Jer. 10:11) .

That one verse was spoken in the Aramaic language, for it would be of less use to speak to the Babylonians in Hebrew. Aramaic, however, was the common trade language employed right across the Middle East; the Babylonians would understand it! By his prophet, God indicated to his people that they should be concerned to speak intelligibly to their captors *and* provided a script prepared in the relevant language.

On another occasion, God gave to the great king Nebuchadnezzar a vision of the future history of the world and Daniel was given the wisdom to interpret that vision:

> You were looking, O king, and lo! there was a great statue. This stature was huge, its brilliance extraordinary
>
> (Dan. 2:31).

Nebuchadnezzar would have liked that speech, especially when Daniel went on to explain that he, Nebuchadnezzar, was the statue's brilliant head of gold.

Sometime later, Daniel was given another vision of the history of the same empires which were still to come but the message was presented in other terms:

> I, Daniel, saw in my vision by night the four winds of heaven stirring up the great sea, and four great beasts came up out of the sea, different from one another.
>
> (Dan. 7:2,3).

To proud Nebuchnezzar, the message came in the form of a statue of a magnificent human being. To a humble servant of God the imagery used was that of wild beasts of prey, for those empires which were to come would be given over to the worship of false gods and the persecution of believers.

In all these examples, and there are more, we have seen that God constantly spoke in a language relevant and meaningful to his hearers, whether they were believers or unbelievers.

Further reflection will doubtless indicate many more examples of God meticulously relating himself to the situation of those to whom he spoke, particularly in the appositeness of the language of God's prophets. But enough examples have been given here to make the valid point that God couched his messages in the most appropriate way *every time he spoke*. Surely we should not ignore the divine model?

In brief

Watch God at work!
The Son of God, and the apostles, certainly did.

To think about

What do you think Paul meant when he said that for the gospel's sake he made himself a slave to all (1 Cor. 9:19)? Is that what we have here seen God doing when he spoke to men and women in Old Testament times? How do I make myself a slave to those to whom I speak?

9.
More of God at work

We have already referred to the statement of the writer to the Hebrews that God has now spoken 'by the Son' or, perhaps, as has been suggested, 'in Son language'. The writer subsequently enlarges that thought:

> Since, therefore, the children share flesh and blood, he himself likewise shared the same things ... he had to become like his brothers and sisters in every respect
>
> (Heb. 2:14,17).

We can look into the Gospel accounts therefore and expect to see God speaking in 'Son language', meaning that Jesus was God veiled in a humanity relevant to those whose flesh and blood he shared in that age and culture. He did not appear as an Indian in Palestine but as a Palestinian Jew.

There can be no doubt that Jesus was uniquely equipped to talk in a relevant manner to the people of his day. John, early in his Gospel account, makes the point that:

> Jesus ... knew all people and needed no one to testify about anyone: for he himself knew what was in everyone
>
> (John 2:24,25).

That is not an expertise we can ever claim to have. Yet there are good ways in which we can, and should, exercise responsibility in this matter of being relevant. We will look at those in later chapters; meanwhile let us watch God at work in the Son.

We saw earlier that Nicodemus, being locked into a culture of physical rituals in religion, stumbled at the thought of being 'born again'. But we need to ask why it was that the Lord Jesus stopped the flow of Nicodemus' preamble by confronting him with the concept of new birth without which no one could even see the kingdom of God. A clue to the answer to that question is found later in the record where we learn that Nicodemus was 'a teacher of Israel', literally *'the* teacher of Israel' (John 3:10).

Nicodemus was rich, a ruler, a Pharisee, a member of the Sanhedrin. The Sanhedrin had a President, a vice-President, and sitting on the President's left, one who was called 'the wise man'. Dean Farrar understands Jesus' use of the phrase *'the* teacher' as possibly meaning:

> Art thou the third member of the Sanhedrin the *chakam* or 'wise man', and yet knowest not the earliest, simplest lesson of the initiation into the kingdom of heaven?
>
> (*The life of Christ:* Farrar)

If this is so, then Jesus was addressing a professor of Old Testament theology who should have known all about Psalm 87:5 '... of Zion it shall be said, This one and that one were born in it'. 'Well, Nicodemus, what do you make of that? *Born* into the kingdom, Nicodemus'. Jesus deliberately challenged the man in the precise area of his knowledge; the challenge was both relevant and, what is more, was designed to expose Nicodemus' ignorance, so leading him into a conversation in which he can be taught.

In John chapter four we find a totally different situation. It is not theology, now, which opens the conversation, but a simple expression of human need and its satisfaction, which this woman knew all about! Although she was surprised that a Jew should ask anything of her, a Samaritan, she would have understood and not been threatened by a request for water. Anyone who has travelled in the heat of the East (it was midday, after all) knows how often such a need is felt. And the conversation moved from there into some of the most profound theological teachings of Jesus (vv. 23-26).

We will be looking in detail at the flow of this conversation in Chapter 15. The skill with which Jesus continually prevented the woman from escaping the thrust of his message is worthy of study as a model to follow. But for the moment it is the relevance of Jesus' opening remark which we notice.

The man who had been ill for thirty-eight years requires a different approach again. Significantly, Jesus 'knew that he had been there a long time' (John 5:6). Dean Farrar comments:

> It was obvious that the *will* of the poor destitute creature was no less stricken with paralysis than his limbs, and his whole life was one long atrophy of despair
>
> > (*The life of Christ:* Farrar).

For that reason, Jesus' question was carefully phrased: 'Do you want to be made well?' or, as Farrar renders it: 'Willest thou to be made whole?' It was a question designed to bring a spark of life to a crippled will. And it brought a gleam of hope, for the man at once began to share the misery of his long years of frustration

Again, in John 6 the words of Jesus arise directly from the miracles the day before the loaves and fishes. 'You ate your fill of the loaves', Jesus began, 'Do not work for food that perishes, but for the food that endures for eternal life' (vv.26,27). And not only was this Capernaum sermon drawn from the miracle that they had so recently experienced, it was also making use of the kind of teaching by symbols that the Jews would have so often heard from their rabbis:

> Those who heard Christ ... must almost involuntarily have recalled similar expressions in their own prophets ... it is clear that much of their failure to comprehend Him rose not from the understanding but from the will ... His saying was hard, as St Augustine remarks, only to the hard.
>
> > (ibid.)

One has only to study passages such as Psalm 19:10; 119:103; Ezekiel 3:1-3 to realise that the symbolic use of 'eating' and 'drinking' was not new to Jewish thought. Other studies in rabbinical writings have found many passages where such symbolism is used to depict personal acceptance of spiritual truth. Jesus was speaking in a way true to the pattern of rabbinical teaching and at the same time relevant to the immediate context of the miracle. There was, in addition, the popular notion that the true Messiah would, according to the legends of their nation, provide them with miraculous fruits, wine and bread. Jesus' sermon could hardly have been more relevant.

In a similar way it can be shown that the parables of Jesus were carefully designed to relate superbly to the detail of Palestinian culture of the time. The parable of the prodigal son, as it is known (Luke 15:11-32), provides a good example. In fact the parable might be more accurately called the parable of the prodigal sons, for it is as much related to the grumbling Pharisees (v.2) as it is to the tax collectors and sinners (v.1).

For the younger son to ask for his share of the property while the father still lived was a shocking thing to do in that culture. The boy was virtually saying, 'Dad, I wish you'd drop dead!' The elder brother should have jumped in and rebuked his younger brother at once, not merely for expressing such a thought but also for daring to go direct to the father and not putting the request through him.

There was provision in Jewish law for the father to draw up a will in which he shared out the property between his sons and let them know of it; but the law stipulated that no property could change hands while the father still lived. That this father gave the inheritance to his young son while he was still alive would have brought gasps of astonishment to Jesus' hearers for there were scribes listening who knew the law!

No wonder the younger son left the village! The villagers would have been furious with him for having so flouted the cultural pattern of village life. The wealth of the village was reckoned to be the total wealth of all the villagers. This son was not merely taking from his own family; he was thereby robbing the whole village. Jesus' hearers would have nodded in agreement. They knew the son would be an outcast in the village if he stayed: he must leave.

Before, and after, the time of Christ a number of famines afflicted the Middle East; no surprise, then, that a severe famine should overtake the young man in the distant country. And carob beans were the common food in famine times when little else was available; the animals had to survive on the bean pods. Again, Jesus' hearers knew all about such hardship. But presently a famished prodigal son 'comes to himself' and struggles home.

> ... while he was still far off, his father saw him and was filled with compassion; he ran and put his arms around him and kissed him
>
> (Luke 15:20).

One thing which a village elder *never* did in those days was to run; his dignity as an elder of the village forbade such an action. Why then does Jesus make this father run? Because he knew, and all Jesus' hearers would have known, that once the villagers spotted this young man at the village boundary they would have hounded him away again. Was he not a disgrace to the village? The father ran so that they two could walk back into the village together, the son under his father's protection.

The son makes his confession. He has sinned against heaven; that is to say, he had kept pigs which was a sin against the holy law and he had also failed to honour his father; that is to say, he had wickedly offended against the Jewish law and disgraced his father, his family and the village. He wanted now to be treated as a 'hired servant'. Jesus' hearers would have spotted the significance of that request. Hired servants did not live on their employer's property but in their own place. Hired servants received a wage — was the son proposing to pay back what he had stolen? Was he hoping to gain favour by his own efforts?

The father would have none of that. 'Bring out a robe — the best one'. Not the son's best robe, of course, but the father's own best ceremonial robe. The son had sold all his robes. Then, a ring for his finger: a sign of belonging again. Sandals for his feet: he was a son, not a servant. The father honoured his son with astonishing mercy and grace.

Now the elder brother appeared; Jesus' hearers recognized him as typical of the grumbling Pharisees (v.2) who would avoid even the shadow of a sinner falling on them. As elder brother he should have been master of ceremonies at the home-coming party. But this elder brother would not even enter the house. To the astonishment of his hearers Jesus tells of the father coming out into the street to reason with this son. It was unheard of that the head of a family should so demean himself before a son; for a son to argue with his father in the open street so that the whole village could hear and see was even worse.

The whole parable is shot through with aspects of the culture of the day; it would alternately have shocked and pleased the hearers for they recognized that this was intimately related to them: they would have been listening avidly to every twist and turn of the story because it was so carefully crafted. They would have noticed that the father's actions showed unearthly graciousness to a sinner, while they recognized the elder brother's contempt for a sinner as the attitude of every

Pharisee. The parables of Jesus, as well as using a common rabbini-cal teaching method, were rooted firmly in the culture of the day. He spoke in the idiom of the people.*

As did the Master, so did his disciples: their preaching always took account of the hearers to whom they preached. We noticed this in Chapter 5 but, in a little more detail, it is relevant here also. If it were a matter of presenting the gospel messages to Jews, the method was to trace the history of God's dealings with that nation, culminating in the coming of Christ the Messiah: whether it was Stephen (Acts 7:2-53) or Paul (Acts 13:16-41; Romans 2:17-4:23) the method was the same. To a people who had the Scriptures, the record of the Scriptures was used. The message was put in terms familiar to its hearers.

If, on the other hand, it was a matter of presenting the gospel to a pagan audience, the method was different; beginning with the fact of creation and the Creator, the theme of the messages moved to the responsibility of the creature to that Creator and the fact of judge-ment to come (Acts 14:14-18; 17:22-31; Rom. 1:16-2:16). To those who had no Old Testament scriptures, the 'Bible' the apostles used was the 'Book of the Creation'. That was a 'book' with which even pagans were familiar.

To the centurion in Caesarea who was described as a God-fearer, Peter spoke within the knowledge the man already had, 'You know the message sent to the people of Israel' (Acts 10:36). There was no tracing through the history of Israel nor was there need to begin from the fact of the created world. Peter spoke of current events in the land with which the centurion and his gathered family and friends would have been quite familiar. He began with what they already knew and built upon it.

When Paul wrote to the believers in Philippi he made use of the fact that their town had a special status. Its citizens were reckoned to be citizens of Rome, with all the privileges, protection and duties which that entailed; Philippi was thought of as little Rome. How meaningful, then, was Paul's comment:

But our citizenship (*politeuma*, A.V. 'conversation') is in heaven ...

(Phil. 3:20).

---

*For a helpful study of this and other of Jesus' parables, see '*Poet and Peasant*' by Kenneth Bailey.

Similarly, Paul earlier writes to these Philippian believers:

> ... live your life (*politeuma*, A.V. 'let your conversation be')
> in a manner worthy of the gospel of Christ
>
> (Phil. 1:27).

'Live your life' (*politeuo*, meaning 'be a citizen') was exactly the right term to use to a people proud of being Roman citizens though living in the colony far from Rome, for believers are citizens of heaven though for a while living far from heaven. Paul was writing with relevance into a specific situation; the church members would have grasped his meaning with delight. They were recipients not merely of the benefits of Rome but now enjoyed far greater heavenly protection, privileges and blessings, and they owed an allegiance not merely to an earthly power but to a heavenly authority. The former was a poor model of the glory of the latter but it was a relevant illustration.

Perhaps some of the most vivid examples of God speaking to his people within the precise details of the situations of their localities occur in the Seven Letters to the churches, as any good commentary will show (Rev. 2:1-3:22). For example, Ephesus was a city with an illustrious past. It lay at the point where three highways met, from the north, the east and the south. It had a good inland harbour. The city was of the greatest commercial importance. The Romans made it a 'free city', granting it the right of self-government and the right to issue its own coinage. In the month of May every year the Pan-Ionin games were held there. It was a city of great religious importance housing one of the seven wonders of the world, the temple of Diana. It is not difficult to see why the city has been called, in William Barclay's phrase, 'The vanity fair of the ancient world'.

But by the time of the letter to the angel of the church in Ephesus, the city was dying. Deforestation had allowed the soil of the steep hills to slip and choke the valley and the river beside which the city stood. Rainfall became irregular. Trade declined. The harbour silted up.

> Hence, Ephesus today; a dead monument to human strife and
> wickedness and man's prodigal treatment of the good and
> faithful earth ... The church at Ephesus was a community in
> a city shadowed by civic death ... It is odd to find the spiritual

reflection of that fact in the Christian church ... in miniature
the story of the church was the story of the town.

(The seven churches: E. M. Blaiklock)

That church had been favoured above many: Paul ministered there
for three years; so did Timothy (1 Tim. 1:3). Apollos, Aquila and
Priscilla, and Tychicus had all ministered there. The apostle John
made Ephesus a centre of his ministry. No wonder the letter speaks
of 'a first love' there! But now the honeymoon period was over. The
church had lost its enthusiasm and passion just as had the dying city.
How relevant, then, both to the city and to the church are those sharp
commands: 'remember ... repent ... and do'.

Situated in such a cosmopolitan city, the church by practical
experience must have developed a keen ability to discern the
character of a person. It is not uncommon for those who live in such
communities to develop a shrewdness in regard to the ways of men
and women. Consequently they had not been led astray from the true
doctrine that was delivered to them.

But living in such a 'vanity fair' brought the problem of separation from immorality, selfishness and general lack of integrity:
hence the presence of Nicolatians. Polite conduct in such a pagan
and commercial society was difficult for believers to observe. For
example, the Christian soldier was duty-bound to salute the regi-
mental standard, which was an idol. The Christian business man
attending a civic banquet or commercial reception was sharing in a
drink offering made to the gods. Buying meat in the market could
mean buying meat once offered to idols. Attending the games
included watching pagan rites.

The Nicolatians solved the problem by arguing that the Christian
was freed from all law and could do exactly what he or she liked. For
them there was really no problem of separation from common city
life. But the church at Ephesus regarded that 'liberty' as licence and
held out against it with holy hatred, though perhaps their icy
correctness had been achieved at the cost of warm Christian love?

The Ephesus letter concludes with the promise of reward:
'eating from the tree of life that is in the Paradise of God'. The
church was abstaining from the doubtful pleasures of decaying
Ephesus; the promise was that of immortality by the pleasant
nourishment of the tree of life. So even the reward related precisely
to the dying situation in which the church found itself.

This has been an extended treatment of one of the letters; the same striking relevance to the contemporary situations of the different churches can be found in each of the seven. The great Head of the church shaped his messages specifically so that they came with force and with inescapable meaning in each particular case to those who had ears to hear.

We looked, above, at the contemporary relevance of the way in which the Lord skilfully shaped his parables. The question might well be asked, why, judging from New Testament records, did none of the apostles use parables in evangelism? Surely they would have been following their Master's example had they done so? Indeed they would not! Jesus used parables because that was a method familiar to his hearers from rabbinical practice and because those whom he taught learned best by pictorial presentation of the message.

The apostles however took the gospel message into the Greek and Roman world where learning was so much more a matter of using syllogistic and logical styles of reasoning, of question and answer dialogue. To have used parables in that context would not have been relevant to the culture* So the apostles, while following the principle of cultural relevance so superbly used by Jesus, rightly used the same principle *but applied it in a different way*. In the Graeco-Roman world they used logical argument, not picture language.

There is also the point to be made that whereas Jesus, before Pentecost, had of necessity to say 'the kingdom of heaven is like ...' and draw a parabolic picture; after Pentecost, when the church as the body of Christ was formed on earth the apostles could say, as also should we, 'Come to church and see the Kingdom of God at work!' Parables of what the Kingdom is like are not so necessary as illustrations now; the Kingdom has come; its beauty should be seen and experienced in the life of every true church. Jesus' parables serve now as standards against which to judge whether the church has 'got it right' or not.

Just once (Gal. 4:21-31) Paul permits himself to use an allegory.

---

*It is still true that some people learn best by a visual approach in teaching; with the huge popularity of television presentations of material today it may be well that less and less people generally will learn easily from logical, linear presentations without visual aids. The Christian communicator cannot afford to ignore that difference of culture.

But the context must be kept in mind. Paul is writing to 'those who desire to be subject to the law' and who are obviously influenced by Judaizing teachers who tried to bring Paul's converts back into Judaism. A Jewish context made this rare Pauline use of allegory relevant. And if it be argued that the letter to the Hebrews contains possible parables, it, too, was addressed to Hebrews.

One last point here: not without significance is the fact that Jesus and his apostles did not hesitate to quote from the Greek Septuagint translation of the Old Testament from time to time. That was the 'Bible' version most widely known across the Greek-speaking world though it was not always the most accurate translation of the Hebrew text. Again, it was a matter of using, wherever possible, what was culturally relevant rather than pedantically insisting upon a version less likely to be understood.

Thus, quickly looking through Scripture in Old and New Testaments, we have found evidence of God's continual concern in love to communicate through his agents in ways which sit accurately and comfortably in the individual contexts being addressed. There is no escaping the conclusion that this is a divine principle, a gracious concession to the sinful human inability to grasp spiritual truth any other way, and it is a challenge to whoever would seek to be a Christian communicator today. There is no way we can honour our Lord and Master if we ignore his careful examples.

In brief

Whether we look in the Old Testament or the New, both confirm that whenever God spoke he did so in ways that used the idiom, the circumstances, the culture of that particular time.

To think about

How relevant to our hearers is our expression of the Christian message?
How well do we understand what would be relevant to them?
How can we tackle the problem of being relevant to all kinds of people?
Remember Paul! To Jews, Gentiles, with/without the law, weak, strong, etc.

Grandma on the beach

10.
Grandma on the beach?

What we have seen as we have watched God at work communicating through biblical histories could be called *acts of transposition*. Transposition means the presentation of something that is originally rich, full of variety, colour and impact, but representing it now in a medium far less rich and full.

Think of a great orchestra creating a magnificent sound, enough to fill a vast concert hall. The gist of the same music, however, could be reproduced in a living room on a single piano. That is transposition: presenting the rich and the full in a comparatively mean and meagre medium. And we are familiar with the idea of transposition in many areas of everyday life. Take, for example, grandma on the beach.

The sun is shining, the sky is blue; one can hear the waves swishing across the shingle, the seagulls mewing, the sound of children playing happily; there is the smell of the seaweed, the softness of the sea breeze, the warmth of the sunshine; the sand, the sea, the sky, the distant white cliffs, the trees, the colours of the beach huts all affect you; every physical sense is drinking in the scene. And there, in her deckchair, is grandma happily knitting. Now you take out your camera and capture the picture — except that your film will only 'see' in black and white.

When you collect the print of your picture, you have what is a drastic transposition. You hold a flat two-dimensional piece of paper which is grey, silent and lifeless. Gone are the three dimensions of the original: gone are the warmth, the sounds, the smells, the colours. That isn't grandma on the beach, is it? Well, it certainly isn't anyone else. But what a transposition!

And every time the high and glorious God of the Bible stoops to speak to the limited human creatures of earth, he has to transpose; the greater has to be put within the poor grasp of the lesser; it has to be a transposition far more drastic than anything involving grandma on the beach. We have already noted the fact that the creation itself is an expression of God's wisdom ad power, which is a fact of transposition that the apostles made use of when addressing Gentiles who were unfamiliar with the Old Testament. But there are other examples, as follows:

Consider the case of the Bible itself which makes the claim to be 'God breathed' (2 Tim. 3:16), a claim which everyone who is awakened to spiritual life by it recognizes to be true. So we have in the Bible a revelation of the thoughts of God himself. Yet those divine thoughts, in our English Bibles, are presented in chains of English words which are shaped according to the laws of English grammar and divided into verses and chapters by an English theologian. But God himself does not 'think' like that.

The eternal, sublime, awesome mind of God does not think progressively for he sees, all at once, the end from the beginning; nor does he need to think in little capsules called 'words', or in chains called 'sentences'. Yet to convey something of his wisdom to us he graciously transposes it to bring it within the limitations of our linguistic ways. Transposition is, therefore, of necessity, a divine principle of communication.

Another example is the case of the Tabernacle in the wilderness. It was carefully constructed precisely according to the pattern shown to Moses on the Mount. And there was a reason for that precision. The Tabernacle, its furnishings and its ceremonies were all to be models of heavenly truth; they were 'sketches of the heavenly things' (Heb. 9:23). As it is said:

> Christ did not enter a sanctuary made by human hands, a mere copy of the true one, but he entered into heaven itself
> (Hebrews 9:24).

So heavenly, spiritual truths were being 'copied' in timber, metal, linen, animals and their skins and by physical rituals; the supramundane was being expressed by means of the mundane, which was an enormous transposition.

Supremely, the Incarnation of Christ is the ultimate in transposition: God, as Man, an all-glorious, infinite Being of unimaginable perfection is presented to us as a Palestine Jew who talked Aramaic and collected the dirt of the earth between his toes as he walked the tracks of the countryside. Such is a transposition beyond our understanding — 'Our God contracted to a span, incomprehensibly made man', as Wesley's hymn puts it.

So, transposition is something which God has used as a communication method. And we need to be eternally grateful that he has, for how else would we ever know anything of him? Only by such a method could anything of heaven's rich glory be brought down to the level of earthlings.

The believer's communication to an unbelieving neighbour is going to involve a similar transposition. The believer has Christ's resurrection life within by the presence of the Holy Spirit. The believer is aware of spiritual experiences which are intellectually and emotionally rich, full, deep and moving, all of which have now to be expressed in some way within the mental grasp of someone who knows nothing of these things. The problem of grandma on the beach hardly compares in complexity! The spiritual message which Christians long to communicate must be 'incarnate' in the ways and words of those who are listening.

Transposition by 'incarnation' is the right way, so long as that phrase is understood carefully. Of Dr. Martyn Lloyd-Jones it has been said:

> He preached to bring the truth to men and to bring men to the truth. His sermons were therefore Christ-centred and people-oriented. He never presented the truth before his hearers (much less out of their reach) with a 'take it or leave it' attitude, but he began where men and women were, that he might bring them where they ought to be. You could call it incarnational preaching.
>
> (Peter Lewis: quoted in *Five Evangelical Leaders:* Christopher Catherwood)

The message must be embodied in a recognizably relevant way to the hearer. This is biblical transposition.

So let us consider a little further what Paul meant when, as we saw earlier, he said that to Jews he became as a Jew, to Gentiles as a Gentile, to the weak as weak, to the strong as strong, by adjusting his way of life and by shaping the presentation of his teaching in

different contexts. In startling words, referring to those Christians
whom he regards as 'weak', he said:

> Therefore, if food is the cause of their falling, I will never eat
> meat, so that I may not cause one of them to fall
>
> (1 Cor. 8:13).

Paul 'chained himself' to the limitations of the weak and worked
within those limits in order to present the gospel message, not
eliminating any of the content of the gospel message (what good
would that have been?) but always presenting that essential content
relevantly. His method might be described as a 'life-style' method
of evangelism. People could 'see' the message in him (Acts 20:18;
1 Cor. 4:16; 2 Tim. 3:14).

We need guidelines to discipline our transpositions. We have
already hinted at that in Chapter 4, for a thing can be transposed so
far from the original as to make it unrecognizable. (There is a
painting by Picasso said to be of female nude which is so far
removed from the form of the original as to be quite safe for public
display without fear of stimulating impure thoughts!) The gospel
messages can likewise be unrecognizable if transposed unwisely.

Helpfully, the guidelines we need are available in the three
examples of what God has done which we examined above. For
instance, no divine transposition has ever resulted in something
being abnormal, odd, freakish or bizarre. The Bible comprises
writings from many different authors at many different periods of
history. There are different style of writing, vocabulary and grammar. The writings all sat comfortably in the cultures of their days.
Emphatically, they are the very words God wanted written; equally,
they are the normal work of human writers. The Bible did not come
into being by any form of unnatural 'mechanical' dictation from
God. Inspiration of the Scripture is a miracle but it did not override
the natural skills of the writers: the end result is not abnormal,
freakish or bizarre.

Likewise the Tabernacle: it did not freakishly rise up out of the
desert sand. It involved donations of materials from the people and the
work of skilled craftsmen. It was obviously man-made, composed of
normal materials available at that time and place, and designed to be
suitable for a desert context and a nomadic people. Yet it precisely
depicted God's truth: it was made according to a divine design.

And the Incarnation? Jesus was obviously a true Jew. He fitted into his day and age — no one ever called him a freak from another age. In outward appearance he matched his brothers and sisters. It had to be acknowledged that there was something about him which was not true of any other but that was *because* he was apparently such a true Jew — his wisdom seemed so unusual for an ordinary Jew.

So the first guideline is that in whatever way the Christian communicator presents the gospel message, through overt witness or daily Christian living, the impression must never be given that there is something out-of-date, eccentric or odd in being a believer. We must be in touch with our context. If we are out of touch, we are odd; if we are odd, we are not biblical.

There is a second guideline arising both from what God has done and what the apostles did in their communicating. There was always a jealous concern that truth was not distorted. We know how God dealt with any of his servants who failed to present the truth accurately; for that reason his people Israel were eventually swept into captivity because of their continual perverting of the truth. Even saintly Moses, who struck the rock when he should have spoken to it, had to be disciplined (Num. 20:12).

And there is no doubt that Paul had a jealous concern for the accurate presentation of gospel truth. Even if it meant an eye-ball to eye-ball confrontation with an important pillar of the church like the apostle Peter, Paul was inflexible!

> When I saw that they were not acting consistently with the truth of the gospel ... I opposed Cephas to his face
> (Gal. 2:11,14).

Paul experienced pain when he saw the gospel being perverted; so must we. No transposition can be tolerated if it misrepresents the truth as revealed in the Bible.

One more important point: there is the possibility of the Christian communicator who seeks to adapt the presentation of the message being misunderstood by fellow Christians. Unfortunately that is a price which may have to be paid. We have already seen how Paul's application of his principle to be all things to all people meant that his behaviour seemed, on the face of it, to be inconsistent (Chapter 4). It seems likely that there were those of the early church who were ready to call him 'the lawless one' (1 Cor. 9:21). Paul protests he is not lawless but is 'under Christ's law'. Nevertheless, the misunderstanding arose in the context of Paul's concern to be 'as' those to whom he spoke: Jew or Gentile, weak or strong.

Christ also knew what it was to be misunderstood. Even his disciples were astonished to find him talking to one Samaritan woman — and in public, too! No self-respecting rabbi ever spoke to his wife in public. And the religious establishment of Christ's day could not accept the fact that he ate and drank with tax-collectors and sinners. Yet, like the good Samaritan in the parable, he was not afraid to 'come where they were' and to present truth in a down-to-earth manner. If we have understood Paul correctly, this must be part of what it means to be 'under Christ's law'.

In brief

Transposition is the key to communication. The message must be embodied within the hearer's limitations but not distorted in the process.

To think about

We transpose when we try to explain adult concepts to small children.
Try transposing some spiritual truth (regeneration, conversion, repentance, justification, sanctification, etc.) for your unbelieving neighbour.

THE PROCESS OF A COMMUNICATION

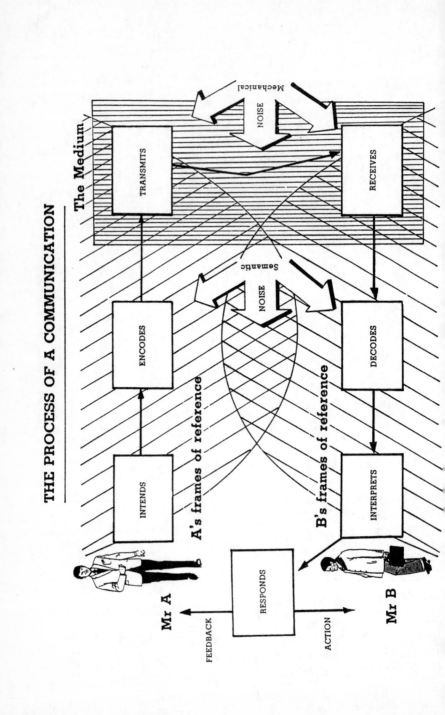

11.
Frames of reference

In Chapter 7 we traced the path of scientific opinion from the 'Bullet' theory through the 'Category' theory to arrive finally at the 'Relationship' theory. In Chapters 8, 9, and 10 we looked at a number of scriptural examples of communication. Certain biblical principles have emerged from these examples. It will be interesting to see how these principles compare with the findings of scientific investigation into how communication works. The biblical examples of communication we have examined always took place in the context of a carefully constructed *relationship*. We are ready to explore the practical implications of this fact, now.

The process of a communication can be analysed into a chain of links, though we are scarcely conscious of proceeding through those links when we talk to someone. Nevertheless the analysis is valuable in exposing the points at which a communication can go wrong and which are, therefore, the points to watch carefully to ensure that it succeeds.

Let us assume that a certain Mr A wishes to speak to a certain Mr B. Mr B at this point is unaware of Mr A's desire which, at the moment, is simply an idea in the mind of Mr A. Nevertheless, Mr A ought to have given the matter some careful thought already. What is his relationship to Mr B? Inferior? Superior? Is he known? A stranger? A different nationality? An enemy? A colleague? Of the same religion or another? All these things and more must begin to shape the *manner* and the *tone* of the approach that Mr A adopts. To get these matters wrong would be to lessen the chance of the communication succeeding even before it has begun.

For example, Mr A will ask his sweetheart to 'Come here' in quite a different manner and tone from that used by a father to a disobedient offspring. The manager approaches the office boy in a different manner from the way in which the office boy approaches the manager. The Christian worker needs to approach the non-Christian differently from the way he approaches a fellow-believer, especially if that meeting is casual or if the non-Christian is of another faith. Right at the outset, relationship is assuming importance.

Hopefully, Mr A has given some thought to the situation and has prepared his attitude. The next step is to put his intended communication into some 'code' which will allow him to transmit his unseen thought to Mr B. There are a variety of 'codes' which can be used to convey a communication. A driver sounds the car horn to warn a pedestrian; an artist paints a picture to express an idea; a musician plays her music to convey her mood; the preacher looks for suitable words to encode his message. We will confine Mr A to words as being the 'code' he must use.

Mr A's choice of words will be influenced by his experience of words for words have two kinds of meanings — 'cold' and 'hot'. Words whose meanings have been learned from a dictionary or from hearing everyday speech can be thought of as being 'cold'. Words whose meanings have been felt in some real life experience can be thought of as 'hot'. You may know that a migraine is uncomfortable from what others have told you or from your study of a medical book, but once you have had a migraine yourself that word will have a 'hot' meaning for you!

To hear a piece of music will sometimes trigger a mental picture of the significant place and circumstances where that piece of music was first heard, making a deep impression upon you. The music has a 'hot' effect, arising from that special circumstance. To anyone else it may still be a pleasant piece but it will not have the same impact on them. For them, as they listen, the music will not have 'hot' associations. The impact of words can vary in the same kind of way.

The 'hot' meaning of a word will have been produced by the 'frame of reference', the life experience, in which the significance of the word has been learnt. Thereafter that word will have a certain force in the consciousness of that individual. The Christian will inevitably talk about the Lord Jesus Christ with a warm emotional understanding because of the experience of knowing Christ in conversion; the words 'Lord Jesus Christ' are 'cold' words to the non-Christian.

This is probably the point at which we need to meet Ben. As a tiny infant, Ben was given a soft, cuddly toy for Christmas. And Mummy and Daddy taught him that the toy was 'a dog'. As he grew older, Ben was given a lovely picture book, on the fourth page of which was a brown shape. Grandad told him that was 'a dog'. Whenever Ben found that page he would make a barking noise to imitate a dog. For Ben, you see, the letters *D O G* were gaining in meaning through his advancing experiences.

As a young lad Ben was given a Yorkshire terrier puppy. Now 'dog' had increased in meaning again; it was alive! It was smaller than Ben, sniffed, wagged its tail and sometimes smelled. Ben decided that he loved dogs; they were fun! However, one day at the seaside Ben and his uncle built a splendid sand castle on the beach, digging a moat around it and making a bridge over the moat. But then a great Alsatian came bounding up the beach from the sea, trampled all over the castle quite ruining it, and shook itself vigorously sending sprays of sea water in all directions. Ben was disgusted; was this also a dog? Bigger than Ben, unpleasant, wrecking Ben's handiwork? Ben's frame of reference for *D O G* had widened, putting new 'hot' meanings into the term. Let's hope he never meets an unfriendly rottweiler!

Ben still needed to experience one more frame of reference for *D O G*. He became a Christian and was accepted for missionary service in India. There in the villages he learnt that the pariah dog is a scavenger. It cleans up filth, can even be infected with rabies, and is generally kept at a distance. Now, at last, Ben's frame of reference for *D O G* is big enough for him to understand why the Bible says there are no dogs in heaven. There is no filth in heaven; the dog, in an eastern book like the Bible, is a symbol for the sort of character which likes to feed on uncleanness and impurity. There is nothing of interest for such characters in heaven.

This has been a grossly exaggerated illustration of frames of reference and their consequences. But it should have made a point: frames of reference can be critical in the matter of successful communication. They can affect the significance we attach to words and will govern the words we choose to 'encode' our thoughts. Mr A's frames of reference will have much to do with the words he eventually uses.

Mr A is now ready to speak. He has to transmit his words so that Mr B can receive them. Transmitting and receiving are the next two links in the chain. Mr A can write, telephone, fax, use e-mail, a microphone and public address system; simply shout, whisper or speak normally. There are things to think about even at this point, you see, to ensure the success of the communication. And again, the method may also have some effect on the manner used. However, the two most important things at this point are to ensure that there is continuity of the medium between Mr A and Mr B, and to guard against distortion of the message by noise.

If the method of transmission is by writing, Mr A must be sure Mr B can read. If the method is by speech, it will fail if Mr B is deaf or if he speaks another language. In Christian communication there may be little or no continuity of medium if Mr B is unfamiliar with 'the language of Zion' which Mr A loves to use; or, what is worse, that communication will convey quite the wrong message. We will look at this problem presently. If Mr B is asleep, speech as a method of transmission will be useless (preachers, note!). There must be continuity of medium used between the two men.

The noise of a pneumatic drill operating alongside Messrs A and B will distort, if not destroy, the message. If Mr B is rushing to catch a bus and cannot stop, that is also a 'noise' factor which will halt the communication. If Mr A is dressed in a slovenly manner and has long dirty hair, he may be just the sort of person Mr B detests; that's 'noise' again, which will damage the success of the communication. If the preacher has a funny mannerism, or a garish tie — or perhaps, in some circles, even no tie at all — the communication may be in peril. 'Noise' which interferes can be of many practical sorts: whatever sort it is, it will hinder the listener from receiving the message correctly.

For our purposes, we assume Mr B has successfully received Mr A's message, or we shall have to stop half way through the process! What Mr B has to do now is to 'decode' Mr A's communication; that is to say, he has to take the words he has heard and draw from them their meaning, thus comprehending the message he has been sent. And the message he will draw from those words will be shaped by the frames of reference in which he — Mr B — experienced those words. That is why frames of reference are such important things.

In order for Mr B to receive the precise message Mr A wishes to send, he must understand Mr A's words *in the same way as does Mr A*. Their two frames of reference must overlap. If they do not overlap, Mr B will deduce a different message from that which Mr

A sent. It is at this point that another form of 'noise' can attack the communication: semantic 'noise'. Our Australian friends call a folding camp-bed 'a stretcher'; our American friends put 'gas' into their automobiles; we put petrol or diesel into our cars. Examples can be multiplied. We met the problem in Chapter 4. Successful communication depends upon overlapping frames of reference, free from misunderstanding arising from semantic 'noise'. Ambiguous words, words in a foreign language, words spoken in a wrong tone of voice, unfamiliar words, words wrongly pronounced, jargon words — these all produce semantic 'noise'.

Mr A needs to realise therefore that the important thing in this whole process is *what Mr B understands*, rather than what Mr A has said. The message actually communicated is not what Mr A said but what Mr B *thought* he said. What a student learns is more important than what a teacher teaches. We have reached the point where the need for relationship is underlined again; how can Mr A know how Mr B will decode his words unless he has a relationship with Mr B which tells him something about Mr B's frames of reference.?

Happily our Mr B has correctly decoded the message from Mr A. So now he acts. On the one hand, he may simply do what Mr A says; or he may refuse to do it: end of communication. On the other hand, he may wish to discuss the matter further in which case, of course, Mr B uses the whole process of the same chain of links — from intention, through encoding to transmitting. And all the things that applied as Mr A spoke, now apply as Mr B speaks in return. Mr B's message can be distorted or lost at all the danger points we identified before. And, again, if there is a relationship between the two men, the danger of mishap is lessened in proportion to the closeness of that relationship.

Obviously, this whole process takes place in a flash. We do not slowly and systematically think through the chain link by link. Indeed, once a conversation has started, the observed reactions of Mr B may cause Mr A to modify his code midway through his message or even to apologize and stop the process altogether. He may have discovered Mr B was not the person he thought he was! But this itemized process must be understood if for no better reason than to identify, and so avoid, points where communication can go wrong. Most importantly, an understanding of the process helps us to see, again, the critical importance of relationship to successful communication. *Relationship* is the key to over-lapping frames of reference.

What we have established now is that the biblical principle — the value of relationship to communication success — is precisely what secular research into the subject has discovered. Biblical principles are not contrary to true science. They make sense! (See Appendix 1).

In brief

The Bible does not need scientific validation in order to confirm its trustworthiness. But it should be no surprise to the believer when scientific research arrives at a biblical conclusion. The same God who created the physical universe inspired the Bible: he will not contradict himself.

To think about

Analyse some conversation which in your experience created misunderstanding in some way. Can you now see why? Does not much popular comedy rely on misunderstandings caused by frames of reference which deliberately do not overlap?

12.
Keeping in touch

In chapter 11 we saw that if two people are in conversation, each having different frames of reference for the words they use, their intended meanings will not overlap. No overlap means that no message has been conveyed — or, what could be worse, the wrong message was received. If our Mr A had used the kind of words recognised by Mr B as the sort of ancient language in which William Shakespeare wrote, it would have been difficult for him to feel that Mr A was exactly 'with it' in today's world. The semantic noise created by the old phraseology would bring a message that Mr A was an oddity and therefore there would be little point in listening to what he said, which certainly was not the message Mr A intended to send.

The apostle Paul made exactly that point to the church in Corinth when he wrote:

> If then I do not know the meaning of a sound, I will be a foreigner to the speaker and the speaker a foreigner to me ... If, therefore, the whole church comes together and all speak in tongues (i.e. sounds whose meaning is not known), will they not say that you are out of your mind?
>
> (1 Cor. 14:11,23).

If the speaker is not understood, the message received by the hearers may be, 'The speaker is not normal'. And this is a danger against which the Christian communicator must carefully guard.

The distinction between the kernel and the shell of the nut illustrates this point. The kernel is valuable; the shell is dispensable. Likewise, the message is valuable; the 'envelope' in which it is conveyed is dispensable. To insist upon sending a message for today in the language of yesterday is to make the shell as valuable as the kernel. There is a tendency for Christians sometimes to feel that the message is only safe if expressed in stereotypes of a past culture. We are not seeking to reproduce the past; to do that is to oppose the will of the Lord who has put us in this day and to shirk our responsibility to struggle to apply the message to our culture.

The more that Christian conversation, behaviour and worship separate off from what is intelligible in everyday life, so the greater is the danger that Christianity will be regarded as not being relevant to today's world. Christian activity will seem to involve mystique, to be engaged in only by an educated elite or by unintelligent persons. The Sunday meeting will become divorced from general Monday-to-Saturday living, since it requires special language and behaviour — sometimes even requiring dressing-up in special robes. The frames of reference of those 'within' the elite circle have then become massively distanced from the frames of reference of those 'without'. How unlike God's revelations of himself! How unlike Christ and the apostles!

Of course there will be some individual biblical truths that will still be expressed by Christians in 'technical' terms. Yet even today the world is not entirely without a knowledge of what slavery is, or what is meant by a need to be saved; wickedness and unbelief are not terms wholly devoid of meaning. And the threat to 'crucify' some-one still has a clear metaphorical meaning at least. So basic gospel truth can be expressed intelligibly in the twenty-first century, even if some doctrines still need distinctive 'technical' terms that will require explanation.

Nevertheless it remains *biblically* important that:

> To fulfil the Christian task of making the gospel available we must make the language and idiom of the worship accessible to the culture of the people we serve. If this is *only* the traditional congregation there will be no need for change. If, however, we want to open the doors of our church and reach out into the culture which is rapidly changing and often alien to traditional religious language, then exclusive patterns of

worship simply won't do. And since we are the 'people of the word' and conveying verbal truths, the wording of our *worship* will require attention first of all.

(Preparing for worship: Michael Perry)

It is worth noticing that when the early church was setting in place the simple structures necessary for orderly church behaviour the apostles did not coin new and 'technical' terms to describe those tasks. Christian jargon language did not originate then. The terms 'bishop' *episkopos* and 'deacon' *diakonos* are used nowadays for officials in churches. Robert Banks, quoting Epictetus, *Dissertationes*, 111, 22:97 and Plutarch, *De Solone*, X1X, 1 writes:

> No real evidence exists to suggest that these terms had any technical meaning at this time (i.e. Paul's day — HJA). This is confirmed by the fact that in the second century Ignatius and Polycarp know of no Episcopal pattern in the church at Philippi ... The word *episkopos* served a wide range of purposes in non-biblical Greek, being applied to men and women overseeing various activities of other people, philosophers examining and testing their hearers and, most relevantly ... office holders in voluntary societies. The term never refers to any precise function. The positions held are always of a minor kind.*
>
> *(Paul's idea of community:* Robert Banks)

In other words, there was no special Christian 'language'. The apostles took and used words from the daily language of the Greek world. The common Greek citizen would have understood when they heard Christians talking. Banks writes further, of the term 'elder':

> In secular Greek 'elder' *presbuteros* simply meant 'senior man'
>
> (ibid.)

---

*Paul writes to the Philippian believers (1:1): 'To all the saints in Christ Jesus who are in Philippi, with the bishops and deacons'. He gives 'the saints' precedence of place in the order, not the 'bishops and deacons'. Clearly there was no rigid hierarchical 'pecking order' in place at that time. The initial emphasis was on being 'ordinary' saints not upon a new Christian officialdom.

The term was ordinarily used of the elders of a city, as for example, in Luke 7:3. Likewise the term 'deacon' *diakonos* had a wide range of meaning, describing many different kinds of helpful service done by anyone — male or female — for others. The term 'church' *ekklesia* had a common civil and secular use as, for example, in Acts 19:39 ('regular assembly'). In all these examples it is as though the early believers were taking great care not to distance themselves from their non-Christian neighbours by using unfamiliar terminology.

It seems clear from the names of those Christians to whom Paul sends greetings in Romans 16 that it was not the custom in the days of the early church for people to change their pagan names to Bible names upon their conversion. Those names of the church members in Rome are quite common Jewish and Roman names. Paul's own change of name from Hebrew 'Saul' to the Greek 'Paul' was not in order to assume a specifically Christian or Bible name:

> His humility induced him to abandon the grand title of 'Saul' (asked for) and assume the humble one of 'Paul' (the little one), appropriate perhaps from his bodily size but adopted, no doubt, from that humility which makes him count himself 'less than the least of all saints, and not worthy to be called an apostle'.
> (*Analytical Concordance to the Holy Bible*: Robert Young)

'Paul' would not have seemed an odd name to the Gentiles to whom he preached. The early Christians were obviously concerned to remain 'in touch' with their unbelieving neighbours.

William Carey, with the others of the pioneering Serampore Three, had it exactly right when they refused to permit their converts from Hinduism to adopt the names of Bible characters. It was argued that this would separate them from their Hindu neighbours in an unnatural way and create an additional barrier to the spread of the gospel message.

There will inevitably be a difference of life-style between Christians and others. But in every possible way it seems biblically right for believers to be as 'normal' as possible in their culture and society. Jesus Christ was, after all, known as 'the friend of sinners'. The gospel message is itself a cause of offence to proud unbelief but that should be the only offence which separates believers from their neighbours. We have the encouragement of knowing that it is the unique work of the Holy Spirit to deal with that unbelieving pride.

For us not to 'keep in touch' to every extent possible creates unnecessary barriers. Our obligation to evangelize compels us constantly to seek to find overlapping frames of reference, which we cannot do unless we 'keep in touch' with our neighbours.

'Keeping in touch' is not a new idea. A second century Christian writer describing the Christian life of his day writes:

> While they dwell in both Greek and Barbarian cities, each as his lot was cast, and follow the customs of the land in dress and food and other matters of living, they shew forth the remarkable and admittedly strange order of their politeia (meaning 'heavenly citizenship' — HJA)
> *(The Epistle to Diognetus, v.4:* quoted in *Seek the Welfare of the city:* Bruce W. Winter)

Another interesting aspect of the apostolic determination to 'keep in touch' with their hearers is demonstrated by their flexibility in the terms they used in which to convey the gospel message. Writing of what he calls the 'evolution of preaching', Kirsopp Lake suggests:

> In the first stage the 'good news' was the coming of the Kingdom of God; this was the message of Jesus himself. In the second stage it was that Jesus was 'the Man' ordained to be the judge of the living and the dead; this was the preaching of the disciples to the Jews. The third stage was the announcement that Jesus was the *kyrios* (Lord) which doubtless ... must have meant much more to heathen minds (i.e. more than the term 'Messiah' — HJA).
> *(The beginnings of Christianity, vol.4:* Ed. Jackson and Lake)

There is no doubt that 'Lord' was far more intelligible to pagan minds than the Jewish term 'Messiah', so much so that the term 'Lord' became a direct challenge to the Roman Caesars who delighted to use that title of themselves. History records how Polycarp was asked, 'What harm is there in saying 'Kyrios Kaiser' (Caesar is lord)?'

At first he made no answer, but when they persisted he
replied: 'I have no intention of taking your advice'
                                        (*The history of the Church:* Eusebius)

Clearly, the term 'Lord' was *very* meaningful in the pagan world: it
brought Christians into direct conflict with the emperors (see 1 Cor.
12:3).

Other terms used to express the gospel message were similarly
'translated' as the ministry of the apostles moved from Jewish to
Gentile culture. The kernel was being presented in different shells.
Michael Green provides examples;

> A phrase like 'Kingdom of God' or 'Kingdom of the heavens'
> is essentially Jewish, and points to the fulfilment of the theo-
> cratic hope longed for by the prophets ... in Israel. But in a
> Gentile milieu it was not a particularly helpful or meaningful
> idea, and was, moreover, liable to be grossly misinterpreted ...
> Accordingly we hear less and less about the 'Kingdom of God',
> though it never entirely drops out, and increasingly synonyms
> replace it, such as 'salvation'. The greatest synonym, of course,
> is Jesus himself. The kingdom is inseparable from the King.
>   (*Evangelism in the early Church:* Michael Green)

The same kind of 'translation' of the terms used in presenting the
message can be demonstrated many times, as Michael Green
illustrates in his book. For example, Paul's use of the term
huiothesia (adoption) is making use of a concept which is not
Jewish but was common in the Roman world in order to convey to
Gentiles how the gospel message brings those who once 'were far
off' into relationship with God, making them 'joint heirs' with Christ.

> Paul's genius as an apologist is his astonishing ability to
> reduce to an apparent vanishing point the gulf between
> himself and his converts, and yet 'to gain' them for the
> Christian gospel.
>   (*New Testament Studies, 'All things to all men'*: Henry
>   Chadwick)

There is our apostolic example! Their message was vital. The
cultural expression of it was adaptable. So we have biblical warrant

for deliberately expressing the content of the gospel in terms which reach the understanding of our hearers; how can we in our speaking of the gospel ignore the force of that apostolic example *for our day and cultural situation?*

Words are not neutral things which exist unaffected by their cultural contexts. They arise in, their meanings are coloured and governed by, the usages of particular contexts and world-views. As we have already seen, it is the message of the words in their context which is important, not their mere form. With the result that:

> the greater the linguistic and cultural distance between the source and the receptor languages, the greater the number and extent of the formal changes required to preserve the meaning.
> (*Christianity in culture*: Charles Kraft)

The message intended by 'Greet one another with a holy kiss' (2 Cor. 13:12) can as well be properly conveyed for an Englishman by 'Greet one another with a warm handshake'; or, for a person in India, by hands held together as if in an attitude of prayer; or, for the Japanese, by a deep bow; or, for a Tibetan, by the tip of the tongue protruding between the lips!

But what if we have no knowledge of those with whom we would share the gospel message? How then shall we translate our gospel presentation into their language — to a stranger, unexpectedly met; to the unknown householder who answers our knock on the door; to the new child in the Sunday school class or weeknight club; to the people passing by our open-air meeting? How can we know what *their* frames of reference might be? We turn to that now.

In brief

Keeping in touch with those to whom we want to explain the Christian message means getting alongside them and understanding their culture.

To think about

What efforts do we make in order that non-Christians can see how we, as believers, live and behave? How are we 'keeping in touch?'

13
Suffer the little children

There are certain things we *can* know about everyone. And there are fairly reliable consequences which we can assume from knowing those thing. For example, there are at least four sets of circumstances which will apply to everyone: their physical situation, their cultural situation, their theological situation, and their spiritual situation.

The person to whom we are speaking is physically a child, a youth or an adult; healthy or in some way unwell; wealthy or poor. Culturally, he or she will be the same nationality as ourselves or different; 'working class', 'middle' or 'upper class'. Theologically, they will be Christian or non-Christian, or of some other faith or cult; theologically aware or ignorant. And spiritually, either alive, or dead; weak or merely curious; agnostic or atheist. It does not take long to 'locate' the person to whom we speak even though sometimes, initial impressions will need to be revised.

Those four frames of reference will act like filters, governing their understanding of what we say, These matters must be borne in mind, therefore, when we shape our approach and our speech. We need to cultivate the skill of 'empathy'. A number of our English words include the ending '-pathy'. Coming to us from the Greek language, the word 'pathy' means 'feeling'. Thus we have 'a-pathy' — no feeling; 'sympathy' — fellow-feeling; 'anti-pathy' — feeling opposed to, and this word 'em-pathy' — to feel *as if you were living 'inside' others*. Empathy is the key to the closest form of relationship and so the best of ways in which to communicate.

We follow a Lord, do we not, of whom it is said:

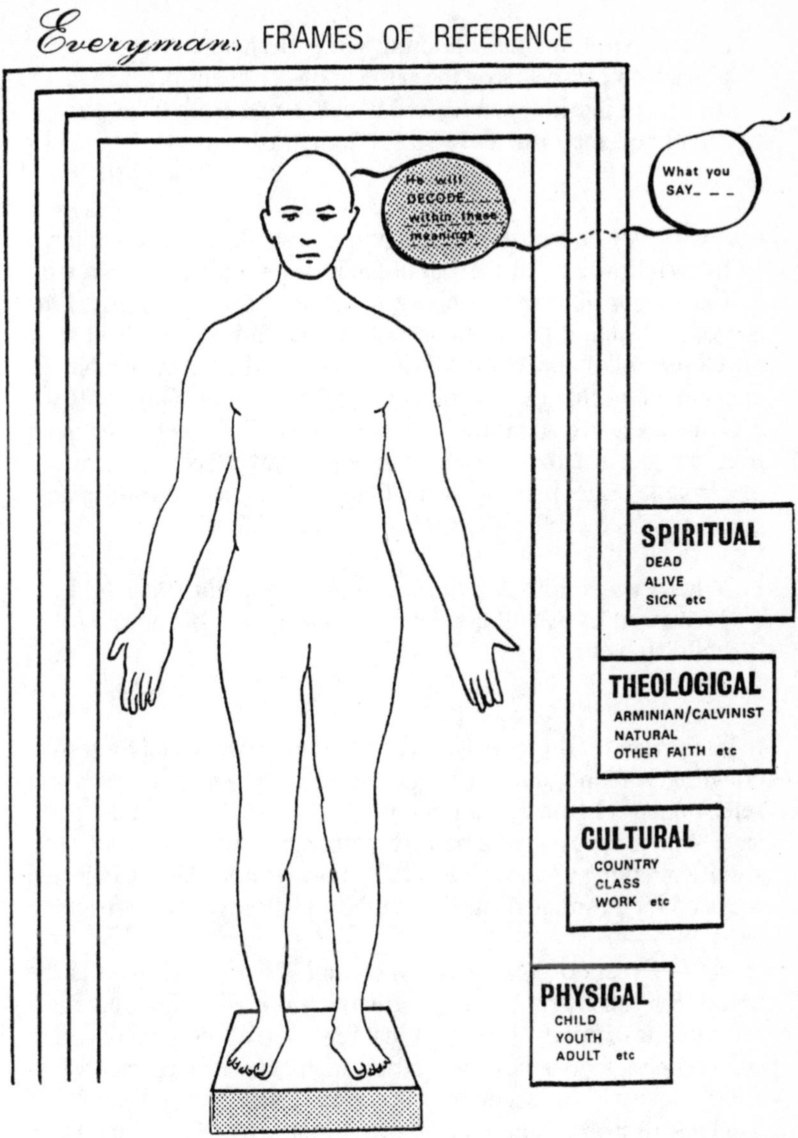
Everyman's FRAMES OF REFERENCE
He will DECODE within these meanings
What you SAY
SPIRITUAL
DEAD
ALIVE
SICK etc
THEOLOGICAL
ARMINIAN/CALVINIST
NATURAL
OTHER FAITH etc
CULTURAL
COUNTRY
CLASS
WORK etc
PHYSICAL
CHILD
YOUTH
ADULT etc

> Since, therefore, the children share flesh and blood, he
> himself likewise shared the same things ... Therefore he had
> to become like his brothers and sisters in every respect that he
> might be a merciful and faithful high priest
>
> (Heb. 2:14,17).

His empathy with us is more complete than anything we can achieve
with our fellows; but it marks out the goal for which we must aim.

Let us consider the teaching of Bible truth to children. Our
approach to children must be tailored according to the natural
development of the child. That which children are capable of
understanding changes dramatically as they develop. Obviously we
must deal here in generalities: children do not all develop at the same
rate, nor against the same background. Nevertheless, there are
discernable stages in the growth of their comprehension and understanding which can be identified.

> When I was a child, I spoke like a child, I thought like a child,
> I reasoned like a child; when I became adult, I put an end to
> childish ways
>
> (1 Cor. 13:11).

In infancy and early years (2-3 years) the child is physically active:
crawling, walking, and enjoying toys; mentally, a discoverer of new
sensations; 'religiously', an imitator — you say 'Amen', the child
says 'Amen'; you put your hands together, the child copies you. The
significant thing of this age is its the short attention span and hence
the need for a continual variety of things to discover, to learn and to
copy.

At 4-5 years of age we see a change. Physically, there is the
ability for constructive and imaginative play. Mentally, there is a
questioning of things — Why? What for? How? 'Religiously', there
is a willingness to believe what they are taught. It is a period when
Bible facts will be accepted — a great time for Sunday School
teachers! But the significant thing of this period is that the child
understands everything literally. There must be no use of figurative
language yet. The earnest preacher talking to the children about sin
did not help their understanding of his message by saying, 'Children, do you know you are all black inside?' That was medically

wrong. biblically wrong, probably an offence against the Race Relations Act, and certainly conveyed the wrong message to the children.

'How does Jesus come into my heart, then?' asked a worried 5 year old; 'Does he cut a hole and crawl in?' What a ghastly caricature of a glorious biblical truth! All because an unwise teacher used figurative language to a youngster who at that particular age could only interpret literally everything she heard.

At the age of 9-11 years new factors come into the child's understanding, Social awareness begins to develop: it is enjoyable to do things with friends. Mentally, figurative language can be handled more easily. 'Religiously', it is a time when a sense of worship begins to appear. The object of that worship is likely to be a T.V. character, a footballer, a musician, or even the Youth Club leader. But the notion of adoration begins to be meaningful; it's a great time for youth work.

By 12-14 years dramatic changes begin — physically and mentally it is the time when adult faculties are emerging. Mentally, they feel they know everything and can criticize everyone else. Socially, it is a time when special friends are selected as distinct from a general group. Interestingly, this is a time when perhaps more spiritual conversions occur than in any other age group. It is as though the whole personality is waking up, coming alive. Now is the time for the challenge of the gospel message, for the apologetic undergirding of the validity and relevance of that message and for emphasis upon the value and reliability of moral and biblical absolutes. It's a great time for the preacher.

These are generalisation; they will not be equally true between children from a Christian home and those from a non-Christian home. Nevertheless, the point needs making that the style of the approach and the content of the teaching needs to relate to the changing child. A serious attempt must be made to put the message within the mental grasp of the child at each stage of its development.

Perhaps the two most critical periods are those of early childhood when you are likely to be believed unquestioningly, and adolescence when what you say is most likely to be challenged. The danger is that if the child has not been able to understand in earlier years, then in adolescence doubt will begin to take over because there has been no intelligible foundation laid upon which belief can rest.

Research among children to study the development of their

thinking about prayer has shown a similar pattern of changing ability of understanding.

> Overall, the results showed a development from 'crude, materialistic, egocentric' concepts to more 'defined, spiritual and altruistic' concepts. Three main stages were delineated. The first, lasting from 7-9 years old, is time-dominated by a concrete materialistic viewpoint. The child has a sense of receiving immediate assurance from God, and material results are felt to be achieved by a process which is somewhat magical ... The second stage (9 to 12 years old) is semi-magical ... God's presence is identified with feelings of peace, happiness and confidence rather than with a magical presence ... Goldman's research was able to identify a further stage, in adolescence. Here, altruistic prayer and prayers of forgiveness and confession reach their peak. The results of prayer were seen much more in terms of the spiritual results of prayer upon the person praying ... and there, Goldman implies, the development of prayer is halted. The last layer of 'adult prayer' has been laid.
>
> (*The psychology of religious knowing:* Watts and Williams, quoting from *Religious thinking from Childhood to Adolescence:* R. Goldman)

Perhaps a reading through these paragraphs seems to make the teaching of children a nearly impossible task! That impression arises from the fact that we have only been looking at the Christian communicator's responsibility to be intelligible. Alongside that we must always keep in mind God's sovereign grace and mercy. Conversions are not produced by mere technical skill, important though those skills are. The realisation of the presence of Christ in the teacher may make a great impact upon the child, and a sensitivity to the promptings of the Holy Spirit in the teacher's mind may override inherent failings. We must not presume upon those things; but they give comfort when we might despair.

And there is always the solemn possibility that, apart from the sovereign work of God, any hypocrisy discovered in the teacher by the child may well negate all that might be achieved by superb technical skills in communicating. Happy is the teacher who can say with Paul:

I declare to you this day that I am not responsible for the blood
of any of you ... for three years I did not cease night or day to
warn everyone with tears ... I did not shrink from declaring
to you the whole purpose of God ... I coveted no one's silver
or gold or clothing ... I worked with my own hands to support
myself ... in all this I have given you an example
(Acts 20:26,31,33,35).

We turn next to the subject of approaching adults; how do we use
their frames of reference?

In brief

It is harmful, even dangerous, to give a child an adult dosage of
medicine. It is equally important to teach children according to their
age and mental ability.

To think about

The child is the 'father' of the man. If we really believed that, would
we need to change what we teach our children by our words and
lifestyle?

14
Grown-ups too

'I am a born again atheist', said the man sitting on a seat near the open-air meeting when spoken to by an eager Christian belonging to the group. Obviously the remark was intended to put an end to he conversation, which it did very effectively! There are certain frames of reference within which adults commonly live and which inevitably affect what they understand from any presentation of the gospel. For example, this 'born again' atheist was almost certainly trapped inside the frame of spiritual death. His view of the situation was that the open-air meeting was an interfering nuisance because he wanted to sit quietly and watch this world go by; he had no interest in the next. But did his use of that phrase indicate some former acquaintance with Christian things?

Perhaps the too eager Christian should have spoken to him initially about the concerns of this life. In other words, to have talked within his frame of reference and to have been sensitive to the fact that the open-air meeting was an intrusion into his immediate wish for a quiet rest would have been a better approach. For a complete stranger to require him suddenly to interrupt his relaxation to discuss something he wasn't the least interested in just then was too much for him to put up with.

As we have already noticed, everyone lives within certain common frames of reference: the physical — the child, youth, adult; the cultural — rural or urban, white or blue collar; the theological — agnostic, humanist, nominal Christian, practising Christian, or follower of another faith; and the spiritual, — alive, sick or dead. Whatever else may be unknown about a person we meet, we can quickly discern these generalities and that knowledge will help us to begin to get within their general frames of reference.

When Paul was being arraigned before the Sanhedrin it was clear that the trial would not be a fair one because the high priest obviously regarded him as guilty even before the examination was begun (Acts 23:1-3). By using the frames of reference of those who were set to judge him, Paul successfully halted that farcical trial:

> When Paul noticed that some were Sadducees and others were Pharisees, he called out in the council, 'Brothers, I am a Pharisee, a son of Pharisee. I am on trial concerning the hope of the resurrection of the dead'
>
> (Acts 23:6).

Since the Sadducees denied any resurrection and the Pharisees believed that there was a resurrection, the council broke up in confusion and disarray, and Paul escaped.

An even more fascinating example of apostolic use of the frames of reference of their hearers is Paul's masterly presentation of the Bible message in his Areopagus address (Acts 17:22-31). He was confronted there by Stoics and Epicureans. And he made use of that fact in a most skilful way in his address. We have preserved for us, in Luke's record of the event, this one detailed example of the apostle's approach to a pagan audience. It is a superb model for us to follow in such a situation.

Paul begins his address not with a text from the Old Testament (for that would not have had any significance to Greek philosophers) but with something they knew well — an altar to a god unknown. And he observes:

> Athenians, I see how extremely religious you are in every way.

The word translated 'extremely religious' has an ambiguous meaning — either 'superstition' or 'religiousness'. Thus Paul does not antagonize his hearers: they can feel at ease with the meaning 'religiousness' while Paul can be comfortable with the thought of 'superstition'; he is not commending their worship. Indeed, the word 'worship' of verse 23 is a word used in the New Testament both of pagan and Christian worship.

That Paul should begin this way is in line with the biblical truth that human beings are religious creatures and must needs worship something, even if not the true God. As Calvin puts it:

> That there exists in the human mind, and indeed by natural instinct, some sense of Deity, we hold to be beyond dispute, since God himself, to prevent any man from pretending ignorance, has endued all men with some idea of his Godhead ... even idolatry is ample evidence of this fact ... when he chooses to worship wood and stone rather than be thought to have no God, it is evident how strong this impression of a Deity must be.
> *(Institutes of the Christian Religion: Bk.1:111, 1-3:* John Calvin)

And it should not escape our notice that Paul is actually using the Athenian's own confession that their worship was one of ignorance; they cannot charge him with being censorious. He is simply quoting their own words back to them.

> What therefore you worship as unknown, this I proclaim to you.

This is more important than it might seem to be on the surface:

> Upwards of four hundred years before, Socrates had been condemned to death by the Athenians as 'a setter forth of strange gods'.
> *(The Ancient Church traced for the first three hundred years:* W.D.Killen)

These are the same words — 'a setter forth of strange gods' — which people were using about Paul's preaching. Clearly this could have been a dangerous situation for him. So instead of claiming to recommend or introduce a new god, he simply claimed to have more information concerning the one they already worshipped. It was a brilliant introduction to what was to follow. Introductions are *so* important to the success of what follows them.

> There is remarkable tact in Paul's seizing on this circumstance: and yet it was perfectly fair and honest ... in other

circumstances it might seem to be presumptuous for an unknown Jew to attempt to instruct the sages of Athens. But here they had confessed and proclaimed their ignorance. By rearing this altar *they acknowledged their need of instruction* (*italics mine* — HJA).

(*Notes on the Acts of the Apostles:* A. Barnes)

As the address develops it is possible to see how Paul is challenging the presuppositions of both Epicureans and Stoics. He is arguing from within their thought patterns, not his. The Epicureans believed that everything happened by chance; that the gods were unconcerned about the world; that the chief purpose of life was to enjoy the highest pleasures. the Stoics, on the other hand, believed that everything was God, including a 'spark' of the divine life which was in everyone and which returned to God at death; that world history was cyclical, every so often disintegrating and then starting all over again in the same ways; that a state of being free from all emotional feeling was the highest human good.

The Epicureans were atheistic materialists; the Stoics were pantheists, holding that matter was eternal. For one,

'everything was a matter of luck; for the other, it was fate'.
(see: *Paul at Athens:* Clifford C. Pond)

To go carefully through the address is to see how, almost verse by verse, Paul is challenging either Epicureans or Stoic ideas, and doing so by presenting them with biblical truth though without quoting a single Bible verse. He is arguing his case to those who had requested to hear it in a way which related specifically to the thinking of those hearers.

The basic thrust of Paul's argument is that what is invisible must be understood by the visible: how can God be like wood or stone, when we — 'his offspring' — are *living* creatures? Our Creator cannot be inferior to what he has created (verse 29). Since God has raised Jesus from the dead, how can we deny that such a God can call us to judgement (verse 31)? Arguing the invisible from the visible was precisely the method of Greek philosophy, from Plato on.

Quoting from Greek poets was also significant. The first of the quotes— 'In him we live and move and have our being' —was from the writing of Epimenides. He was the poet who it is thought first suggested the erection of altars to an unknown god (*The Acts of the Apostles:* F.F.Bruce). Moreover the statue of Epimenides was there on Mars Hill directly below where Paul was standing if, as is possible, the court was meeting on that site. By this quotation Paul was proving himself a credible witness, showing his audience that he was as knowledgeable and as cultured as they were. Here was a man worth listening to. (Remember the Communication contract, Chapter 7.)

Paul could acknowledge (Rom. 2:14-16) that even Gentiles without God's law had within them some sense of the true God. Natural religion contains glimmers of truth. But acknowledging that fact is far from asserting that pagan religion is true religion. Paul could never, and did never, do that, even though he quoted from pagan poets.

Nor was he implying that the thinking of pagan poets was valid as a guide to the true God by quoting from Epimenides and then, secondly, from Cleanthes' *Hymn to Jove* — 'we too are his off-spring'. (The same words also occur in a writing by the highly regarded Aratus, a Greek poet, a native of Cilicia. Perhaps that is how Paul was familiar with the quotation?) He was in fact using their own poets to show the Athenians that their idolatry was ridiculous. Cleanthes was also a Stoic; Paul was 'becoming as a Greek to the Greeks; as a Stoic to the Stoics'. But none of this was to suggest that those poets knew Paul's God. Indeed, Paul carefully makes the point that they were only vainly 'groping for God, even though God was close to them' (verse 27).

As the address closed the hearers divided into two groups: some were curious ('We will hear you again about this'); others scoffed. Perhaps this confirms the division of the hearers into Stoics and Epicureans. But there were some who believed. As to the long-term results of the address, Conybeare and Howson (*The Life and Epistles of St Paul*) suggest that there was still a church prospering in Athens in A.D.165 and which was later represented in the Council of Nicea in the forth century. They also comment:

> That speech on Areopagus is an imperishable monument of the first victory of Christianity over Paganism ... It is in Athens we learn what is the highest point to which unassisted human nature can attain, and here we learn also the language which the Gospel

addresses to a man on his proudest eminence of unaided strength.

It has been suggested that Paul was regretting what he had done in Athens, regarding it as a failure, when he commented to the Corinthian church that:

> I decided to know nothing among you except Jesus Christ, and him crucified. And I came to you in weakness and in fear and in much trembling. My speech and my proclamation were not with plausible words of wisdom
>
> (1 Cor. 2:2-4).

Such a suggestion is an assumption based on little evidence. The 'words of wisdom' which Paul was rejecting were words of worldly wisdom; the Areopagus address was continually rejecting worldly wisdom. To declare nothing among them 'except Jesus Christ' was exactly what he had done in Athens; they knew he was talking about Jesus in the market place, which was precisely the reason they asked him to Areopagus to hear more. And in Acts 17:31 Paul obviously confronted his hearers with the resurrection of Christ, clearly indicating that Christ had died.

> There is nothing in Paul's own words in 1 Corinthians to suggest a change of plan; rather, he intends to describe his normal practice, though this normal practice was bound to appear more striking in a place like Corinth. He is not contrasting his evangelistic method in Corinth with that which he employed elsewhere, but with that which others employed in Corinth.
>
> (*The first epistle to the Corinthians:* C.K.Barrett)

This has been, deliberately, quite an extended study of Paul's address to hearers who were ignorant of the Bible; for exactly such are those in our society today whom we must address with the message of the gospel. Paul gives us a superb model to follow — a model which is wholly consistent with both the biblical and the scientific principles we have studied. Who of us will be Pauline, as we seek to tell the Truth today?

In expressions markedly courteous, and with arguments exquisitely conciliatory* ... enforcing his views by their own poets, he yet manages, with the readiest powers of adaptation to indicate the fundamental errors of every class of his listeners. While seeming to dwell only on points of agreement, he yet practically rebukes in every direction.

(The Life and Work of St Paul: F.W.Farrar)

In brief

Paul went to those who had no Old Testament as one who himself had no Old Testament; yet his sermon was thoroughly biblical.

To think about

Many around us today are more pagan than Paul's Greeks. They have no sense of religion at all and no knowledge of the Bible. Since it is the *message* of biblical truth which is to be conveyed, can we express that message biblically without quoting Bible verses, as Paul did?

---

* In his *Studies in Preaching*, Vol.2, Jay E.Adams makes the point that when Paul reacted to the idolatry he found at Lystra (Acts 14:6-16) he 'lost his composure as well as his audience':

The words 'tore their clothes ... rushed out ... shouting' cannot be dismissed. Was Paul a 'Lycaonian to the Lycaonians' when he tore his clothes? Was he not rather a 'Jew to the Lycaonians' by this act? This seems to have been a reversion to his Jewish heritage.

In contrast, although Luke is careful to point out Paul's indignation at the idolatry of Athens ('deeply distressed' — Acts 17:16) the difference in his address here is in the control over his inner feelings. In Lystra he met idolatry 'head-on'; here, his control gave him a listening audience, and converts. A point worth considering, surely?

15.
Not in my back yard

If Paul had not already told us so, we would surely soon learn by experience that the natural human reaction to the truth of God's message to us is to refuse it. Paul speaks of those:

> who by their wickedness suppress the truth
>
> (Rom. 1:18).

Even in the Old Testament, and referring to the people of God's chosen nation, the prophet has to cry out in anguish:

> Who has believed what we have heard? And to whom has the arm of the LORD been revealed?
>
> (Isa. 53:1).

Lack of interest and even outright rejection of the Bible message is not new. Except in times of the unusual presence and power of the Holy Spirit men and women happily refuse to receive the gospel message. We long for and pray for the Spirit's convincing power, but in the words of William Carey from his celebrated *Enquiry into the obligations of Christians to use means* (1792):

> We must not be contented however with praying, without *exerting ourselves in the use of means* for the obtaining of those things we pray for. Were *the children of light,* but *as wise in their generation as the children of this world,* they

would stretch every nerve to gain so glorious a prize, not even imagining it was to be obtained in any other way.

(*The Strict Baptist Historical Society Bulletin,* No.19, 1992)

The question then becomes, what means are to be used when the Christian message is rejected? Which brings us to consider certain common techniques of evasion which are practised when our hearers wish to avoid accepting our message. To have some idea of those techniques can help us to forestall them or to block 'escape routes' which unwilling hearers can use. Experience shows that it is generally difficult for a radical message to be accepted by people who are not already in favour of the views expressed. People commonly evade points of view which are at odds with their own.

Several evasion techniques are commonly used, the first of which we have already noticed in Chapter 5: the message is made invalid because of previous presuppositions. For example, Nicodemus stumbled over the concept of being 'born anew'; the Samaritan woman failed to grasp the significance of 'living water' for she could only think in terms of buckets and ropes. Another vivid example is recorded for us in the account of Paul's defence before the temple crowd:

> Then he said to me, 'Go, for I will send you far away to the Gentiles'. Up to this point (literally: up to this *word;* the word 'Gentiles') they listened to him, but then they shouted 'Away with such a fellow from the earth'

> (Acts 22:22).

Jewish presuppositions concerning Gentiles that they were unclean, God-forsaken 'dogs', produced in Paul's hearers a bitter misunderstanding of the glory of his message. God had chosen that nation in order that they should be his messengers to the world. Instead, they proudly supposed that they alone were God's people, so much so that now just the one word 'Gentiles' was enough to spark off a riot. Similarly, when we speak to unbelievers their presuppositions often distort our message. So we need to have some idea what their presuppositions are which, in turn, means knowing their circumstances in order to avoid our using 'trigger' words which will give them an excuse to avoid our message.

Another way to avoid accepting a message is to invalidate it by claiming to be an exception to the need for it. It could perhaps be admitted that what is said may be true for some people: others need such a message — but not me! The spirit of the Pharisee who thanked God that he was not like other people (Luke 18:11) is still abroad in the world today. Many still respond to the Christian message with surprise that it should ever be thought that they need it: 'Surely we are not blind, are we?' (John 9:40)

Religion in general and Christianity in particular have been dubbed 'the opium of the people' meaning simple, uneducated people, of course, not those with the 'wisdom' to coin that phrase! We must counter this by providing evidence that there is no one without a need for their Maker's instructions. The Utopian dream of a perfect world without injustice, without violence and without disharmony has been with the human race for centuries. Is not the longing for something better the evidence that we are all conscious of a need? But why has the 'better' never come? Is it not because the Maker's instructions are ignored?

Then again, a further way to avoid a message is to change the frame of reference of the message: when Jesus spoke to the woman at the well (John 4), she reminded him of their national differences — Samaritan and Jew. Jesus countered this by implying that he was One who was above human nationalities, capable of giving more than common water. The woman challenged the right of Jesus to talk as though superior to great Jacob of old. Jesus countered this by repeating in greater detail how superior his gift of living water really was compared with Jacob's water.

The woman continued to demonstrate that she was locked in an unspiritual frame of reference which could only think in earthly terms. Jesus countered this by a sudden shift of subject to her husbands. The woman attempted a denial but Jesus exposed that for what it was. At last the woman was compelled to realise that Jesus was no ordinary human being. And Jesus persisted in steadily reasoning with her, *blocking off every change of argument,* until the woman came to admit the possibility of his being the God-sent Messiah.

Yet another evasion technique is to declare the message too difficult to understand:

> When many of his disciples heard it, they said, 'This teaching is difficult; who can accept it?
>
> (John 6:60).

Sometimes this particular aversion to accepting the message may be due to genuine educational limitations on the part of the hearer. It can also be due, though it never should be, to an irrelevant and therefore unintelligible presentation of the message. But more often than not it springs from an unwillingness of the mind of the hearer. 'I cannot accept the idea of Creation in six days', said the scientist, 'because I do not want to believe in God'. That unwillingness, rather than any real evidence, pushed him into accepting instead the theory of Evolution. He thereby exposed himself to the inadequacy of his own reasoning; his unbelief was due to a lack of will and not to real evidence; which is a strange way for a scientist to talk. Evidently some scientists have presuppositions too.

The unwillingness of the non-Christian to accept the gospel message of the grace of God to the ungodly (Romans 4:5) arises from the natural persuasion people commonly have that they are autonomous beings, self-governing and independent. The very first sin was committed because that goal of autonomy was the desire of the first man and woman:

> But the serpent said to the woman, 'You will not die; for God knows that when you eat of it your eyes will be opened, and you will be like God, knowing good and evil' ... she took of the fruit and ate, and she gave some to her husband who was with her, and he ate
>
> (Gen. 3:4,5,6).

It still remains true that this pride in being like little gods, masters of our own souls, is an instinctive human feeling. To be faced with the fact that the only hope of heaven is to cling nakedly to the possibility of the grace of God towards us through Jesus Christ is too humbling a proposition to be welcomed by us. Be careful, Christian, how you tell people that 'if you believe, you will be saved'. To a hearer who believes that he or she is the master of their own life, you may be doing no more than encouraging the notion that their salvation is entirely up to them whether they choose to believe or not. You have helped them to evade the fact that in God's sight they are helpless, hopeless, hell-deserving rebels, blinded by Satan, with no freedom of spiritual choice at all.

Lying behind all these techniques of evasion are certain very human factors. For example, there is a general fear of being isolated, of appearing odd. We naturally like to be accepted by our peers as one among them. No man is an island — and very few want to be; nearly everyone wants 'to belong'. So that to evade a message which threatens to isolate us from our peers is a form of defence mechanism, protecting our self-confidence. A crowd draws a crowd, we say; full chapels possess a credibility and attraction which tiny congregations lack. The whole matter of personal relationship and friendship becomes very important in overcoming this natural fear of isolation.

Additional to this fear of isolation are the inconsistencies in daily life which we have continually to negotiate. For example, we compartmentalise our thinking; Sunday habits in one compartment and weekday habits in another.

> There exists in our society a culturally conditioned habit of evasion, a product of the fact that each individual is compelled to participate in many different groups, each of which has its own more or less well defined value systems. Often these value systems are somewhat inconsistent with each other; sometimes they imply a different hierarchy of values.
>
> (*The evasion of propaganda:* Cooper and Jahoda, quoted in *The process and effects of mass communication:* editor W. Schramm)

The children of a Christian family may well be taught the importance of moral values at home. In school and college and in the industrial world, however, they will instead be confronted with the supreme importance of effectiveness in competition, of self-assertion, and of a certain ruthlessness — the 'rat race'. The conflict between those two value systems is often evaded by keeping them in separate mental compartments. Even to think about any reconciliation between the two value systems may be too uncomfortable and hence unwelcome. Only those with strong personalities or those closely supported by others of the same Christian persuasion can be radical enough to resolve such conflicts.

We have also to keep in mind that an accurate understanding of the Christian message is only possible when it is seen as part of a consistent whole. Any one Bible truth is only rightly understood within the full framework of all Bible truth. For example, the proper 'weight' of any biblical statement can only be grasped if it is understood against the truth that 'all Scripture is inspired by God' (2 Tim. 3:16). As a consequence, the significance of what we say to non-Christians (or even to Christians) is very dependent upon what grasp they have of the whole matrix of biblical truth. We may have to start a long way back from where we eventually hope to get if we are to prevent our hearers evading, by inaccurate understanding, the message we most want to give. We must start where they are in their ignorance.

There is one circumstance in which our hearers may be more open to receive a message which is contrary to their own beliefs. A time of changing environment or changing circumstances, is such a time of openness. We have already seen that the teenage years are a time when statistically many conversions take place (Chapter 13). Going to college can be the crossroads when the student experiments either by tasting previously forbidden non-Christian 'delights' or else by, for the first time perhaps, being confronted with a lively Christian group. Such new circumstances can alter previous convictions and result in changes which humanly speaking would not have happened in that person's life.

Tragedies in life, collapses in supposedly secure fortunes, experiences of unhappy situations from which one has previously been shielded, severe illness, disappointment at promises not being realised are all circumstances of change in which former presuppositions may be severely challenged and even demonstrated to be false. These are moments when there may be more willingness to receive a new message. Happy is the believers who can, sensitively and with understanding, come to such a person with the right message just then. But once again, at the risk of being boringly repetitive, the need for a good relationship between the messenger and the hearer is obvious.

On the other hand, life's tragedies and disappointments may produce a bitter and angry reaction: *if* there is a God of love, how could he allow this to happen to me? That is a reaction as old as Epicurus (342-270 B.C.) who put the same question neatly:

Is God willing to prevent evil, but yet not able? Then he is impotent. Is he able, but not willing? Then he is malevolent. Is he both able and willing? Whence then is evil?

(From Hume's *Dialogues concerning Natural Religion*, quoted in *The Enlightenment:* Open University, Studies 11)

The Christian has no need to be afraid of Epicurus's questions. They are well answered by the sad record of Genesis 3 and by what happened at a place called Golgotha some centuries later. By the rebellion of unbelief evil entered the world; by the cross of Christ God demonstrated he was neither impotent nor malevolent but a Saviour from evil to all who will come to him.

In brief

Efforts to evade the thrust of the biblical message are clear evidence of the spiritual death of a soul; they should not surprise us but are to be wrestled with.

To think about

Consider the various ways in which God 'wrestled' with his chosen people through the Old Testament history. Compare our efforts to wrestle with unbelievers today.

16.
Is religious knowledge real knowledge?

When you go to the doctor, you want him to treat the disease and not just alleviate the symptoms. If the present disease of Modernity (and its offspring Post-modernity) in our culture and society arise from some of the rationalistic philosophers of the Enlightenment period of history, as was suggested in Chapter 5, then it is that thinking we must challenge more than the fruits of it which we see around us today. We must go for the germ, not merely attack the symptoms. Kill the germ and the symptoms will vanish. Treat the symptoms only and the germ will live on to appear again, perhaps with new symptoms.

The secular argument which emerges from the discoveries of the Enlightenment period is that reliable knowledge can only be that which is detectable by scientific test. Any other 'information' is merely speculative — subjective feeling or personal opinion, neither of which can be confirmed by any objective test as true knowledge. Since God is invisible and cannot be subjected to laboratory tests, how can we truly know that he exists? Since the universe functions as one great magnificent machine, a splendid closed system of comprehensive causes and effects, who needs God anyway?

The problem has been put very vividly:

> Two explorers, one a believer and the other a sceptic, come across a clearing in a jungle in which many flowers and weeds are growing. The sceptic queries the believer's asser-

tion that a gardener must tend the plot, demanding of the believer that *empirical expectations be stipulated and that tests be made. They set up a watch, they encircle the clearing with an electric fence, they patrol with bloodhounds. But they see no one, hear nothing and the bloodhounds never give an indication that a scent has been picked up. As the empirical expectations are unfulfilled one by one, the believer qualifies his original assertion, maintaining first that the gardener is invisible, then that he is intangible, then that he is inaudible, etc., until the sceptic finally exclaims in exasperation: 'But what remains of your original assertion? Just how does what you call an invisible, intangible, eternally elusive gardener differ from an imaginary gardener or even from no gardener at all?'

('Gods' — *Proceedings of the Aristotelian Society:* John Wisdom, quoted in *Theology and Meaning:* Raeburne S. Heimbeck)

There are several flaws in the conclusions of this parable. The first is this: it is being suggested that 'an invisible, intangible, elusive gardener' means exactly the same thing as 'an imaginary gardener' or 'no gardener at all'. But it does not follow that the former necessarily means the same as either of the other two; there *could be* such a thing as an invisible, intangible and therefore elusive gardener existing outside this physical, empirical world of ours. That there is not, is precisely the thing to be proved and the parable does not prove that.

Other flaws in the parables conclusions are:

1. the suggestion that empirical expectations are the only way to prove the truth of a statement
2. the suggestion that empirical evidences will be adequate to validate, or otherwise, statements about God.

Those two suggestions are both assumptions; they are not proved in the parable. There may be other than empirical ways to prove some

---

*'Empirical expectations' simply means tangible evidence obtained by observation and experiment, as distinct from conclusions obtained by mere theory.

kinds of statement true, which is what the believer can demonstrate. And to say that 'an invisible gardener' and an 'imaginary gardener' or 'no gardener at all' must all mean the same thing, i.e. denial that there is any gardener, is poor logic. Aristotle would be ashamed of it! 'An invisible gardener' is not the same thing as 'no gardener'.

There is absolutely no need for the believer to feel intimidated by the likes of Wisdom's sceptical explorer. Professor Heimbeck amply demonstrates the unwisdom of John Wisdom. Nevertheless the view that religious knowledge cannot be real knowledge is a view which will be commonly met by the Christian communicator today; a view arising from some of the philosophers of the Enlightenment. Religious knowledge is dismissed as subjective and wishful thinking. For example:

> Man strives after happiness and harmony. He finds in himself only weakness, so he projects an all powerful God. He looks to himself and finds mortality, and, because he finds a desire for immortality, he projects an immortal life in heaven. He feels alone and small, so there arises a desire for a godly father. He feels unloving and searches in heaven for a perfect love. Man gives a character of reality to his own deepest wishes.
>
> (*The essence of Christianity:* Ludwig Feuerbach)

> Everywhere, when man is religious, he is so because he suppresses his deep need for protection, his desire for absolute authority, even his feeling of guilt toward this absolute authority.
>
> (*The future of an illusion:* Sigmund Freud)

These quotations suggest that religious knowledge is an invention of the human mind, incapable of any empirical proof and therefore not real knowledge. Disillusioned by fallible fathers and by a sense of our own weakness and frailty, we human beings 'project' our need for strength, reliability, and love into the form of an infinite father on the screen of an imagined heaven. Religious knowledge is dismissed as merely speculative thinking and not regarded as true knowledge.

Of course, not all the unbelievers we meet will have reasoned their rejection of Christianity by means of the logic of atheistic philosophers. Nevertheless, their unbelief is nurtured by such philosophies imbibed almost unconsciously from the atmosphere of a secular culture and its continual media publicity. To destroy that culture we must attack the thinking from which it has arisen. And the tragedy is that we can add to the strength of their conviction that religious knowledge is meaningless if, in our witness and worship, we speak in an unfamiliar, anachronistic way.

There are three lines along which we may refute the challenge that religious knowledge is meaningless. There are psychological arguments, philosophical arguments and biblical arguments.

First, a brief outline of the psychological and philosophical arguments. It can be pointed out that it does not follow that suppressing a need for something means that the object you think you need does not exist. Indeed, the need of which you are psychologically aware may be the very evidence that such a reality does exist. If the object of a felt need did not exist, how would we ever be conscious of a lack of it? Is it not arguable that the concept of God is not a projection based upon felt need, but rather the dim echo of a truth we have lost? That, of course, is the biblical view.

Moreover, if God is merely a projection of the human longing for security, then in precisely the same way it can be argued that atheism is no more than the projection of a human longing to be autonomous and so not to be embarrassed by a God to whom we might be accountable. In other words, atheism is the product of a proud and rebellious human mind which does not want the discipline of having a Master — which, again, is the biblical view.

To argue philosophically that knowledge cannot be true unless it can be discovered by empirical means arrogantly overlooks the possibility that all knowledge is not of the same sort. Allowing that God, not being human, could have properties unique to the divine nature of his being, is it not possible that knowledge of him is also unique and so unlike other knowledge? Before arguing that what empirical tests do not detect cannot be true knowledge it must be established (not assumed) that there is only one kind of knowledge. The Bible, for example, speaks of a knowledge which comes 'by faith' in a God who transcends his creation.

Concluding his exhaustive study of philosophical arguments for the existence, or otherwise, of God, Professor Swinburne comments:

One who has had a religious experience apparently of God
has, by the Principle of Credulity*, good reason for believing
that there is a God — other things being equal — especially
if it is a forceful experience

...The only way to defeat such a move is to show that it is
significantly more probable than not that there is no God ...
unless we take perceptual claims seriously, whatever they are
about, we shall find ourselves in an epistemological (*the
theory of how we know things* — HJA) Queer Street. Religious perceptual claims deserve to be taken seriously as
perceptual claims of any other kind.

(*The existence of God*: Richard Swinburne)

In other words, my testimony that there is a God from what I
perceive as my experience of him, cannot be logically dismissed by
an atheist unless he (or she) can first show they have exhausted
absolutely every possibility that there *might* be a God — an
impossible task. My perception that there is a God can be as reliable
as my perception that there is a table in my room.

Moreover, to maintain that true knowledge is only that which is
capable of empirical proof is to deny human experience. It may well
be that a lover's kiss can be empirically analysed and defined as 'the
mutual transmission of microbes and carbon dioxide',* but human
experience *knows* that a kiss can be far more than that.

A man must live in reality, and reality consists of two parts:
the external world and its form, and Man's 'mannishness',
including his own 'mannishness' ... two things cut across
everyman's will — the external world with its structure, and
those things that well-up from inside himself.

(*The God who is there:* Francis Shaeffer)

---

*By the Principle of Credulity Professor Swinburne means that 'what one seems
to perceive is evidence that it is probably so, but how things seem not to be is not
such evidence.' It is notoriously difficult in logic to prove, beyond all doubt, a
negative.

*Quoted by David Langford, in '*Where is God in all this?*'

So it is not *proved* that all knowledge is of one kind necessarily validated by empirical evidence alone. In any case, empirical knowledge can never answer the question, 'Why'? It can only examine *what* exists. A different kind of knowledge is required to answer the question, 'Why?'

But it is, secondly and chiefly, to biblical arguments I want to turn. That the concept of God is a projection created by a human sense of need is vigorously opposed in the Bible. For example, it is repeatedly asserted that faith in God, as the Bible understands it, is based upon the historical facts — memorial stones were often used as hard evidence of historical fact:

> When your children ask in time to come, 'What do these stones mean to you?' then you shall tell them that the waters of the Jordan were cut off in front of the ark of the covenant of the LORD
>
> (Josh. 4:6).

> Then Samuel took a stone ... and named it Ebenezer, for he said, 'Thus far the LORD has helped us'
>
> (1 Sam.7:12).

In the New Testament, similarly, there is continual insistence upon the historical basis for faith in Christ. The first four verses of Luke's Gospel make that claim. Defending himself before King Agrippa, Paul does not hesitate to argue for the genuiness of the facts of the life of Jesus Christ as being generally known and accepted, even by non-Christians:

> I am speaking the sober truth. Indeed the king knows about these thing, and to him I speak freely; for I am certain that none of these things has escaped his notice, for this (the life of Jesus — HJA) was not done in a corner
>
> (Acts 26:26).

Concerning the death and resurrection of Christ, Paul can confidently assert their historicity on the grounds that:

> Christ died for our sins ... that he was buried, and that he was raised on the third day ... and that ... he appeared to more than

five hundred brothers and sisters at one time, most of whom
are still alive, though some have died

(1 Cor. 15:3-6).

The apostles Peter and John both argued for the historical reality of
Christ and the facts of the gospel message:

We did not follow cleverly devised myths ... but we had been
eyewitnesses of his majesty. For he received honour and
glory from God the Father when that voice was conveyed to
him ... 'This is my Son, my Beloved' ... We ourselves heard
this voice come from heaven, while we were with him on the
holy mountain

(2 Peter 1:16-18).

We declare to you ... what we have heard, what we have seen
with our eyes, what we have looked at and touched with our
hands ... we declare to you what we have seen and heard so
that you may also have fellowship with us

(1 John 1:1-3).

The Bible will not tolerate the idea that religious knowledge is
merely a projection of human longings with no basis in fact.

Furthermore, biblical prohibitions against making and worshipping of any form of idol are a further blow against the notion that
religious knowledge arises from subjective human desires. The
Israelites were sternly forbidden to make for themselves any imaginary god.

Since you saw no form when the LORD spoke to you at Horeb
out of the fire, take care and watch yourselves closely, so that
you do not act corruptly by making an idol for yourselves, in
the form of any figure — the likeness of male or female, the
likeness of any animal that is on the earth, the likeness of
anything that creeps on the ground, the likeness of any fish
that is in the water under the earth. And when you look up to
the heavens and see the sun, the moon, and the stars, all the
host of heaven, do not be led astray and bow down to them and
serve them

(Deut. 4:15-19).

The Psalmist brings a charge against the religious thinking of Israel in no uncertain terms, expressing God's detestation of their sinful worshipping a projection of their own wrong theology:

> You thought that I was one just like yourself. But now I rebuke you, and lay the charge before you. Mark this, then, you who forget God, or I will tear you apart, and there will be no one to deliver
>
> (Ps. 50:21,22).

It must be clear from such Bible statements as these that faith — Christian faith — does not depend upon what we *feel* about God nor upon what we might *desire* God to be for our benefit but upon what God has revealed about himself both in the Scriptures, the written Word, and through Jesus Christ, the living Word. Religious knowledge is not speculative and purely subjective; it is knowledge with a basis in revealed fact. *And this is a point which the Christian communicator must constantly emphasize in the climate of today's secular culture.*

The way in which the fearful doubting disciples were so transformed once they had met the risen Lord Jesus is a vivid conformation that the Christian faith has basis in fact. That Jesus would rise again was light years away from their expectations once they saw him dead.

> We had hoped that he was the one to redeem Israel. Yes, and besides all this, it is now the third day since these things took place
>
> (Luke 24:21).

Yet from that state of depression and despair they became men of astonishing courage and energy in spreading the Christian faith — a change hardly likely to arise from a mere projection of wishful thinking. Such a change could only have come from an unshakeable conviction of the truth of the resurrection of Jesus.

> No body of men or women could persistently and successfully have preached in Jerusalem a doctrine involving the vacancy of that tomb without the grave itself being physically vacant. The facts were too recent; the tomb too close to that

seething centre of oriental life. Not all the make-believe in the world could have purchased the utter silence of antiquity, or given the records their impressive unanimity. Only the truth itself, in all its unavoidable simplicity, could have achieved that.

(*Who moved the stone?:* Frank Morrison)

The fact of the resurrection of Jesus was the cutting edge of all apostolic evangelism and the inspiration of their worship and daily living. And it must also be so for the Christian communicator now because the resurrection is the one piece of evidence for the veracity of the gospel message which God has held out, and still holds out, to the world for consideration:

He has fixed a day on which he will have the world judged in righteousness by a man whom he has appointed, and of this he has given assurance (A.V. margin: 'or, offered faith') to all by raising him from the dead

(Acts 17:31).

Christian faith has its roots in irrefutable facts: they validate the message. That is a first line of defence against the charge that religion is speculation.

There is one more point to be made. Christian faith involves knowledge of a Person: of God in Jesus Christ. No one would want to argue that knowledge of another person is obtained by weighing them, measuring them, and subjecting them to analysis in various chemical tests. Knowledge of another person comes by relationship and love; lovers know each other by the love-reaction between them. Such knowledge is different from scientific knowledge but no less real.

Interestingly, faith-knowledge as we might term it (the conviction that the biblical message is truth), is as much a matter of being known by God as of our knowing him. It springs from a relationship with God. The experience of that relationship confirms the message. For example:

Anyone who loves God is known by him

(1 Cor. 8:3).

Formerly, when you did not know God, you were enslaved to beings that by nature are not gods. Now, however, that you have come to know God, or rather be known by God, how can you turn back again?

(Gal. 4:8,9).

We have already seen how communication on the horizontal level — person to person — thrives in a situation where there is a bridge of relationship and trust (Chapter 7): it is equally true that communication in a vertical sense — we and God — also matures into assured faith-knowledge by relationship. The knowledge of God is a love-reaction based upon historical fact not simply upon an exercise of human reason nor upon a projection of human desire. Even on the human level, knowledge of another person is something gained by relationship not by laboratory examination. Knowledge of God is similarly known by our relationship with him as we know him in Jesus Christ.

And such a vertical relationship is nurtured by a knowledge of the Scriptures where we discover that from its beginning to its end there is the one consistent message (which itself is a remarkable fact given the time-scale of its composing and the variety of its writers) explaining so accurately why our world and our human nature are the way they are, and conveying teaching which is so eminently suited to our life in such a world. The Christian communicator has an armoury of arguments with which to challenge the secular unbeliever and should be able to use them with familiar ease. The Apostles certainly did!

I am indebted for some of the material in this chapter to papers on *'The reality of God'* by Wim Rietkerk in a symposium entitled *'What in the world is real?'* published by L'Abri Fellowship, 1982.

In brief

The historicity of its facts and the accuracy of biblical revelation are valid grounds for asserting the reality of Christian truths.

To think about

This thing (basic universal humanitarian values — HJA) ... which others may call Natural Law or Traditional Morality ... is not one among a series of possible system of values. It is the sole source of all value judgements. If it is rejected, all value is rejected ... The effort to refute it and raise a new system of value in its place is self-contradictory. There never has been, and never will be, a radically new judgement of value in the history of the world.

(*The Abolition of Man:* C.S.Lewis)

17.
Some plain speaking

Arguments rage about translations of the Bible in contemporary English and about hymns in today's English with music in a modern style. Sometimes feelings run so high that fellowship between believers is damaged, which is sad. In the light of all that has been written so far about biblical principles of communication, what can we say about various Bible translations and contemporary songs? Are there ways of reaching conclusions as to what is biblically acceptable?

For example, can we draw a distinction between what is used in a meeting of believers and what is used in evangelistic outreach to unbelievers? Can we apply the biblical principle of adaptation to the unbelieving hearers' understanding, while retaining in the meeting of believers archaic and traditional patterns of thought and expression with which we are so familiar. For example, 'Authorised' version of the Bible in Sunday services, 'Good News Bible' in evangelism?

There is some justification for the argument that if a group is known to be of elderly believers, for example, whose memories are full of the Authorised Version, then the principles we have been studying require us to speak within *their* frames of reference. The same would be true in the choice of hymns used. But it has to be acknowledged that this specific kind of meeting is steadily disappearing as a new generation arises. The approach must be different in a group where young families are growing up.

The society around us is changing fast; no longer can it be assumed that there is a basic knowledge of gospel facts and Christian language in people's minds. Not merely do today's children not attend Sunday school, their parents did not either. We face frames of reference which have no comprehension — or, worse, even a wrong understanding — of Christian thought. And young people in Christian circles need to know how to express the truth to their peers.

Inevitably those who come from that society, whether brought into the gatherings of Christians or reached in their own homes, start from a position of ignorance of Bible truth difficult for established believers to grasp. For the Christian message to be meaningful to such newcomers it must be put into plain speech.

Mrs Brown had been asked to attend an evangelistic service in the chapel. And to the delight of those inviting her, she came. But she knew none of the hymns or the tunes — 'Abide with me' wasn't chosen. All around her people sang enthusiastically; she felt exposed and obvious for she could not join in. Things got worse with the Bible reading: who on earth was Hosea and where does one find what he — or was it she — wrote? They gave a page number, but she felt patronised by that: was she the only one counting through the pages like a child? And why did the minister use 'Thee' and 'Thou' and 'didst' and 'wilt' in his prayer but not in his sermon? Mrs Brown never came again ...

It can be argued that it was too large a leap for Mrs Brown to come straight from her world into a traditional Christian world; it would perhaps have been better if she had first joined a 'Starter group' or an informal 'House Bible study' and thereby come more gradually to the traditional meeting. But doesn't that very admission illustrate the fact that the traditional meeting is steadily removing itself from meaningful contact with daily life? Would it not have been better to have used plainer language in the meeting, which would not only have benefited Mrs Brown but would also have been immensely helpful for the children growing up in the church families? When children do not understand they 'switch off' by reading their book, drawing on their paper, or inventing imaginary games. What have we taught *them* about the Christian message when that happens?

Moreover, if the Christian meeting is not a place where plain contemporary speech is used, how will the participants in the meeting ever be trained to approach unbelievers in evangelism themselves? They will have no example from which to learn. Paul is clear on this. Pastors and teachers have the responsibility:

> to equip the saints for the work of the ministry, for building
> up the body of Christ, until all of us come ... to maturity, to the
> measure of the full stature of Christ
>
> (Eph. 4:12).

This is not merely a reference to the need for the teaching to be biblical in content; it applies as much to the need for the manner of the teaching to be biblical so that the saints are equipped to speak to those outside the meeting.

It does not really seem a valid distinction, then, to separate the language of Christian worship from the language of Christian witness. In any case, the defence for a distinctive worship-language is so often based upon what is merely human tradition and not biblical usage. The argument that the pronouns 'Thee' and 'Thou' are rightly used in worship because they give honour to God cannot be defended biblically, or culturally, in today's world. It is the practice in some world languages to address God with a form of pronoun normally reserved for familiar friends rather than a form reserved to indicate respect for a higher authority. Are such believers being disrespectful to God? And while, in the past, the use of 'thee' and 'thou' was common in general English, it is no longer so:

Thee: pronoun. Objective (accusative, dative) case of Thou; dialect and among Quakers occasionally used for Thou.

Thou: pronoun. 2nd person nominative singular pronoun (now archaic or poetic) denoting person addressed.
(The Oxford Illustrated Dictionary)

Thee, thou, thy and *thine* were once forms of address to express a special relationship to human as well as divine persons. These pronouns are no longer part of our daily language. In addition to the pronoun usages of the seventeenth century, the *-eth* and *-est* verb endings ... are now obsolete ... should we use *love, loveth,* or *lovest*? *do, doeth, doest,* or *dost*? ... the real character of the Authorised Version does not reside in its archaic pronouns or verbs or other grammatical forms of the seventeenth century.

(from The Preface of the *Revised Authorised Version*)

There is no special pronoun used of God in the Bible; the pronoun *su* ('you', translated 'thou' in the A.V.) is the common Greek pronoun of the second person and is used figuratively of places (Matt. 2:6), by John of Jesus (Matt. 3:14; 11:3), by Jesus of his disciples (Matt. 6:3), by a disciple of Jesus (Matt. 16:16), and by Jesus of God (Matt. 17:25). In any case, the translators of the Authorised Version had no problem, apparently, about even using 'thee' of Satan to express the vocative form of his name in the Greek text (Matt. 16:23). 'Thee' is not exclusively kept for God. Compare 1 Cor. 15:55 (AV), 'thy sting', 'thy victory'.

> It should be pointed out that in the original languages neither the Old nor the new Testament makes any linguistic distinction between addressing a human being and addressing the Deity.
>
> (To the Reader, Preface to *The New Revised Standard Version*)

Clearly, there is neither cultural *nor biblical* justification for the use of an archaic English pronoun when addressing God. However, in a special situation where this archaic usage has been the lifetime practice of a group of older believers, as envisaged earlier in this chapter, there is an argument for keeping within their frames of reference. But with the gradual dying out of their generation, that argument will no longer be applicable. What is inconsistent is to mix archaic and current forms in the same prayer.

There is an argument that the preservation of the old forms 'thee' and 'thou' is necessary as in the Authorised Version of the Bible in order to indicate the fact that what is being said is in the singular, to an individual; whereas 'ye' and 'you' were then kept for a plurality of hearers being addressed, a distinction which is lost if 'you' is used both as a singular and plural form. However, the argument looses its force nowadays; in contemporary language no such distinction exists: 'ye' has dropped out of use as archaic and 'you' is happily used both as a singular and a plural pronoun. 'Ye' and 'thee' are understood now as either irrelevant archaisms or as a form of mock seriousness, both good reasons for not using them.

On the other hand, sermons based on Philippians 2:12-13 (AV), for example, have often given the impression that Paul writes there to individuals, even though it is the 'you' form of English pronoun used. In fact, Paul is addressing the whole church, the plurality. Yet so accustomed have we become in using 'you' as a *singular* form that the old plural connotation escapes us even when we do use the Authorised Version of the Bible. The old distinction is lost in today's common practice. But it is a loss which we cannot repair simply by retaining the old, now meaningless, form 'ye'. Instead, the preacher must do his homework and discover whether the pronoun in the *Bible* languages is singular or plural (or find a good commentary that will indicate which it is!).

The unhelpful use of the seventeenth century pronouns must be coupled with other words which have either changed their meaning over the years or have completely dropped out of use. Even when a Bible version is based upon what is argued to be the most authentic Hebrew and Greek manuscripts known, there still remains the solemn responsibility to ensure that the English translation now conveys its message clearly, or there is little value in translating from even the best sources.

> It was in order to make it clear enough for ordinary people to respond to it, that Wyclif and later Tyndale risked their lives to reclaim the Bible from the Latin language into English. If your religion affects the whole of your life, then its language must be that of everyday life, and all the more if you try to reach out and tell the gospel to outsiders who have had little contact with Christianity.
>
> (*Bible translations and how to chose between them:*
> A.S.Duthie)

The writers of the original Bible books were inspired by God to use particular words in their sentences which were meaningful to their current hearers and readers. Our evaluation of any Bible translation should be on the basis of whether it is at once both accurate *and currently meaningful.*

> Too often, even today, the word of God seems to people like a blunt instrument which makes a heavy but unclear impression upon them; rather than as something 'alive and active, sharper than any double-edged sword which cuts all the way through to where soul and spirit meet, to where joints and

marrow come together, and which judges the desires and thoughts of man's heart'

(Heb. 4:12, *Good News Bible*).

(ibid.)

Consider also the fact that in recent years we have witnessed the rise of feminist movements, some strident and secular and others arguing for a right biblical expression of feminism. The question has to be asked as to how communications into this cultural situation. The Bible does use the word 'man' on many occasions when the meaning clearly is not that women are excluded. Hymns frequently speak of 'man' in a way which obviously includes women. Is it not odd, to say the least, to hear a preacher in today's western society refer to a mixed congregation (I once did!) as 'All sons of Adam'. And is it a helpful thing to ask ladies nowadays to sing:

Behold th'amazing gift of love
The Father hath bestowed
On us, the sinful sons of men,
To call us sons of God.

(Scottish Paraphrases)

If it was the cultural situation in bygone days which held ladies in the background as second-class members of a male-oriented society, is it right to maintain that situation in a culture which is now so different? (In New Testament times, to be an heir one had to be a son; it is not so now). Or if it was a recognised thing that 'Man' (Upper case 'M') meant 'all man*kind*' obviously including ladies, but that this use has largely disappeared today, is it good to insist upon using 'man' for 'mankind', what it is no longer used to mean? This is in no way to capitulate to secular feminism or even to pander to evangelical feminism. Quite apart from the cultural aspect of the matter, there just is no biblical justification for excluding ladies from the translation of many Bible statements. The word often translated 'man' (*anthropos*) in our Bibles:

is used generally of a human being male or female, without reference to sex or nationality, in distinction from God and from animals.

(*Expository Dictionary of New Testament words:*
W.E.Vine)

> It is used universally with reference to genus or nature,
> without distinction of sex, a human being whether male or
> female ... distinguished from beings of a different race or
> order: from animals, plants., etc.: from God, from Christ as
> divine and from angels.
>
> (*Greek-English Lexicon:* Grimm/Thayer)

In other words, '*anthropos*, man' is commonly used in Scripture
with a generic meaning. It refers to men and women equally. Why
can we not plainly say so? Other Greek words for 'man' exist which do
specify masculinity. But the noun 'man' nowadays commonly only
means 'the male'. In the context of today's culture such usage is neither
biblically true nor practically wise. The Bible was not originally written
for men only, except in those passages which specifically reflect the
historical situation of an ancient patriarchal culture.

The term '*adelphos*, brother', occurring frequently in the New
Testament, had a common usage in those days meaning 'all members of the same community'. (The word literally means 'of the
same womb'). Its Old Testament equivalent ('*ah*, brother') similarly
could be used for members of the Hebrew community. This community sense of the words obviously includes ladies as well as men.

> *adelphos*: a fellow-believer, united to another by a bond of
> affection; so, most frequently, of Christians, consisting as it
> were but a single family.
>
> (*Greek-English Lexicon:* Grimm/Thayer)

As W.E.Vine comments in his *Expository Dictionary of the New
Testament Words*, 'brothers' is used of believers apart from their
sex; in other words, there is every justification for often translating
the word as 'brothers and sisters' since that is the sense the writer
was often conveying originally. (The word is used some 174 times
simply as a term for 'Christians'; *Theological wordbook of the
Bible:* A.Richardson.)

Moreover:

> During the last half century ... many in the churches have
> become sensitive to the danger of linguistic sexism arising
> from the inherent bias of the English language towards the

masculine gender, a bias that in the case of the Bible has often restricted or obscured the meaning of the original text.

(To the Reader, Preface to *The New Revised Standard Version*)

If we are not to restrict or obscure the meaning of the Bible in communicating its truth to men *and women* today, are we not under obligation to say what it really says in plain language? If the passage means 'men and women' why not say so? This is not to come down to secular levels; it is rightly to represent biblical truth in a culture where 'men' has come to mean male alone, excluding women. To use a wrong word can be a way of hiding a truth.

And what about our singing? The subject of music in worship is a subject for the next chapter. But a few comments about words are perhaps in order here, under the heading of plain talking. It cannot be right to behave as though only that which was composed in past centuries is the gift of God to the church. Has the church only a past, and no present or future? There are believers today who have the gift of expressing spiritual truth in contemporary words. That is not to say that every modern composition is acceptable; that was not even the case with hymns in past centuries. Poor compositions have always properly fallen out of use. There always needs to be discernment about what we sing in worship, for what we sing often shapes what we believe rather than the reverse.

It is not only that traditional hymns are often written in an archaic style of language; sometimes the expressions used are too obscure to be easily understood. What exactly are worldlings doing when they are fading ('Glorious things of thee are spoken')? What is the celestial day which is poured (sic!) on the eyeballs of the blind ('Hark the glad sound, the Saviour comes')? What is a guerdon ('Art thou weary')? Why should it be only Christians men who can rejoice at Christmas ('Good Christian men, rejoice')? Examples of unfortunate phrases can be multiplied.

As to the content of songs and hymns:

We should ask five questions about the words of what we sing in worship:

1. Are the words true — is this what the Bible teaches?
2. What does the song mean — is it clear?

3. Is the song rational — are the feelings it expresses properly rounded in truth?
4. Does the song have a point and purpose — does it make us think meaningfully about what we are singing?
5. Is the language pure — does the song use language correctly and to its best advantage to speak to and about God?

(*What should we sing?* Grace Magazine, April 1995: Nick Needham)

The hymnology of past ages often used figurative language, biblical symbolism and sentence structures in ways which are foreign to our patterns of language today; their use now may only imply that worship in song has to be in old-fashioned words and ideas. Yet, on the other hand, contemporary songs can be found which are no more than mindless repetition of single phrases, or which express 'spiritual' feelings in such exotic language as to make them quite as foreign to common experience as old-fashioned symbolism. Oh, for plain language!

A well-known actor became famous for his one-man performance in which he recited the whole of the Gospel of Mark with no other stage scenery than a chair. It was a brilliant performance. When asked by a puzzled interviewer why he chose to use the old King James Authorised Version of that Gospel, he replied: 'Because of the music of the words'. And he was right. The literary skills with which the translators made that version such a master-piece of translation are undoubted. But what do we wish our hearers today to notice about the Bible — the music of the words or their radical meaning? To ask the question is surely to answer it!

Adherence to old forms of language as the only proper language is not a phenomenon unique to certain people today. In his satirical essay entitled 'The Ciceronians', Desiderius Erasmus (1469-1536) vigorously defended his attempts to perfect a contemporary form of Latin to make it a living language. The Ciceronians, against whom he wrote, were so devoted to the language of Cicero (106-43BC) that they would use no word or phrase unless Cicero had used it.

They reject with intolerable arrogance any literary work which does not reproduce Cicero's stylistic characteristics. They keep the young from reading other writers, restricting them to the meticulous imitation of Cicero as their only model.

> (Quoted in an Open University recording of *The Ciceronians.*)

By means of an imagined conversation between a Ciceronian and a contemporary person (himself?) Erasmus ridiculed the attempt to take Latin usage back to the past, instead of making it a contemporary language.

It may even be that one of the reasons why some Christians feel such a sense of shock when asked to read a modern Bible version or sing contemporary song is precisely because the meaning of the words has suddenly leapt out and clamoured for attention; safely shrouded in old and traditional forms the truth was not nearly so stark, being so much more comfortable to bear, or even ignore. Without plain language we are in danger of smothering the radical message of Jesus in a kind of linguistic cotton wool. We shall have failed to communicate the *biblical* message. Even worse, we shall have failed rightly to represent the true nature of the kingdom of heaven. It is a serious thing to make the understanding of the message more difficult than it already is, in the nature of the case. Isn't that a form of adding to Scripture?

Why has the principle of 'accessibility' required revision of Bible versions and liturgy? Here are some answers:

1. Language changes its meaning with the passing of time.
2. Our 'image' of God should be contemporary as well as historical.
3. Faith and reality should not be divided in people's thinking.
4. A 'private' language makes for an exclusive church.
5. Casual affirmations about God suggest casual beliefs.
6. Evangelism, education, memorability, all require clear statement.
7. All-age worship emphasises this need.
8. Involvement and spontaneity demand an easy identity with the language of worship.

> (*Preparing for worship:* Michael Perry)

In brief

We have no obligation to cling to any supposed 'language of Zion' in our worship and witness; it can even be a denial of our obligation to spread the Christian message *to all* if we do so. Many will not understand that 'language'.

To think about

William Cowper's hymn 'There is a fountain filled with blood' is full of rich Bible truth, but expressed in language crowded with symbolism so extreme as to be strange today. Being plunged into a fountain of blood is hardly the way to lose stains. Does not this modern version express the same truths more slowly, more clearly and even more accurately?

> Our sin is cleansed by blood alone —
> drawn from Immanuel's veins:
> this shall for all our sin atone,
> and cover all its stains.
>
> The dying thief from guilt was free
> by Christ's shed blood that day —
> and still may I, as vile as he,
> wash all my sins away.

> (William Cowper 1731-1800: Revised, 'Praise Publica-
> tions' ©1996)

18.
Facing the music

The song of Lamech is the first song preserved in Scripture (Gen. 4:23,24).

> It is a song of revenge and self-redemption; God's honour is neglected.
>
> (*Pop music*: G.J.Nijhof in *Reformed Music Journal*, Jan.1990)

That so early in biblical history, while Adam and Eve were still alive, a song was composed which expressed hatred and pride is symptomatic of the fact that human nature by that time had already been spoiled by sin. Arising from the rebellion of Adam and Eve, unbelieving mankind had ceased to express delight, thankfulness and honour to God (which surely Adam and Eve must have done before the Fall), wishing instead to be equal with God, autonomous and free from obligation to God. Thereafter, mere subjective human taste is not a reliable guide to whether certain kinds of music are good or bad (or anything else) because human tastes are not exempt from that original cancer of sin. Unguided human ideas must not be taken to be the norm of what is good.

We look, then, for principles by which to discipline our unreliable tastes, thinking primarily here of music in Christian meetings, though the same principles should also guide us in the choice of any music to which we listen for pleasure. Our pleasures, as believers, need to be 'united with the fear of God and the common needs of human society', as Calvin put it. Such guiding principles are essential for:

> We know by experience that singing has great force and power to move and influence the heart of men to invoke and praise God ... among other things adapted for men's reaction and for giving them pleasure, music is either the foremost, or one of the principal; and we must esteem it a gift of God designed for that purpose ... there is scarcely anything in this world which can more turn or bend hither and thither the ways of men ... when melody goes with it, every bad word penetrates much more deeply into the heart.
>
> (*Preface to the Psalter:* John Calvin)

First, music has *power*. When Saul was mentally disturbed:

> David took the lyre and played it with his hand, and Saul would be relieved and feel better, and the evil spirit would depart from him
>
> (1 Sam.16:23).

> Elisha said ... Get me a musician. And then while the musician was playing, the power of the LORD came upon him. And he said, 'Thus says the LORD ...'
>
> (2 Kin. 3:15).

Second, music is an *expression of human moods and emotions*. When Job was grappling with the problem of why he, a righteous man, should be suffering so much while the wicked enjoyed prosperity and musical merriment, he complained:

> Why do the wicked live on, reach an old age, and grow mighty in power? ... They sing to the tambourine and the lyre, and rejoice at the sound of the pipe
>
> (Job 21:7,12).

In contrast, Job suggests that sad, depressing music better represented his condition:

> My lyre is turned to mourning, and my pipe to the voice of those who weep
>
> (Job 30:31).

Isaiah made the point that when God's judgements strike, music stops:

> The mirth of the timbrels is stilled, the noise of the jubilant has ceased, the mirth of the lyre is stilled
>
> (Isa. 24:8).

Quite plainly, when likely to be affected by music expressing human emotions and when being exposed to such a source of power, believers are under obligation to guard themselves from spiritual (or physical!) harm, whether in the Christian meeting or in private relaxation.

Paul speaks of believers expressing the fullness of the Sprit by, among other things, 'singing and making melody to the Lord in *your hearts*' (Eph. 5:19). 'The heart' in biblical understanding means the whole person — the intellect, the emotions and the will. Paul is not here suggesting that the believer should only make music silently and inwardly for the context is that of a church fellowship; nor is he suggesting that believers must always sing heartily or in a rousing manner. He is, however, saying that the believer should be able to use a godly mind, sanctified emotions and a humble will in all musical expressions of worship. Believers are to realize what they are doing when they make music; they are to be careful, thoughtful and intelligent, and sensitive to the meaning of the words.*

The power of music arises from its volume, rhythm, and pitch. All three of these factors can effect the human nervous system favourably or adversely. As to the first of these:

> The body's autonomic nervous system (which regulates such involuntary responses as heartbeat, temperature, digestion, and respiration) begins to react at 70 decibels, equivalent to the sound of traffic on a relatively quiet city street. At that level, vasoconstrictive effects were noted — narrowing of the arteries which raises the distolic blood pressure ... as the intensity of the sound increased the effects grew stronger: dilation of the pupils, dryness of the mouth and tongue, loss

---

*This paragraph owes much to a sermon of Dr M. Lloyd-Jones, November 29th, 1959.

of skin colour, contraction of the leg, abdomen and chest muscles, sudden excess of the production of adrenaline, stoppage of the flow of gastric juices, and excitation of the heart. These effects were automatic, unaffected by the subject's health, his annoyance, or whether he was accustomed to noise on his job. Noise is most dangerous when it is loud, meaningless, irregular and unpredictable.

(*We're poisoning ourselves with noise*: J Stewart Gordon: *Reader's Digest* February, 1970; see also *Music and Communication:* Terence McLaughlin)

On the other hand, soothing and gentle music can be used to quieten patients with certain mental handicaps, and to provide a relaxing atmosphere for restaurants, aeroplanes, dental and doctor's surgeries and sometimes for certain shops. In other kinds of shops and in some factory situations a more strident and obtrusive type of music is used in order to stimulate rather than to soothe. Writing in *The Musical Quarterly* (1994) in an article entitled 'Music Therapy', Doron K. Antrim comments that 'music can affect a person whether or not he is aware of it'.

As to the power of rhythm, some of the physical effects are obvious. Music in march-time sets people's feet tapping or their bodies swaying in rhythm with the tempo. We like what appeals to our body rhythms — breathing rhythms, heart-beat rhythms, walking rhythms, for example. We are 'comfortable' with 50-90 beats minute. What is slower than this 'feels' sad; what is faster 'feels' exciting. An irregular beat, or confusion of beats at one time, produces tension.

The human brain receives musical information in the form of electrical impulses in the same way as it receives information about all our sensory experiences. The brain seeks to recognize the message of music in the same electrical terms of the other experiences it knows such as pain, relief, excitement, fear, sexual, etc. So different rhythms can produce, or in the case of performers *express*, different human emotions. In using music as a form of therapy in mental hospitals it was found that:

the personality of the performer seemed to exert a definite influence upon the response of the patient.

(*Music and your emotions:* L. Gilman and F. Paperte)

In other words, the beliefs and personalities of the performers affect in a discernible way the music they choose and *their* manner of performing it. Both express their emotional state. In which case, ungodliness in the performer can have an influence upon the hearer because the music is an expression of an ungodly mind.

In the case of the pitch of a piece of music, an upward movement of the melody suggests passion or triumph; a downward movement, comfort or resignation. Music in a minor key often (but not always) suggests sadness; a major key suggests normality, satisfaction or gladness.

A number of serious attempts have been made to define what is good music, whether of classical or popular styles. From those attempts certain common factors do emerge. For example, good music will contain a variety of changes in volume which give it character and colour. These changes in rhythm and tempo will give the music 'life' and 'shape'. Good music will have a well-developed melody which gives it movement, and also points of conclusion or rest. Good music will sometimes use changes of pitch and key in order to stress some point of significance and alert the hearer to it.

Good music will be identified by the fact that there is a careful balance between the forcefulness of each of these factors; no one factor will dominate the others. There will be delightful variety but the parts will always be held in mutual balance. We know that variety and balance are found in all the acts of God. The created universe is a model of variety in balance. The ways in which God has revealed his truth through the centuries are so various — history, poetry, wisdom literature, prophecy, formal discourse, letters — yet all blend in harmony. And since we are made in his image we do our best when we copy his balanced ways.

Suppose that today for breakfast you eat nothing but cake, for lunch nothing but candy, and for dinner nothing but pie with ice cream. Tomorrow you have candy for breakfast, pie for lunch and the cake for supper. Now just suppose you kept up this 'diet' for two or three weeks. At the end of that time you would not only be so sick and tired of sweets that you would never want to see them again. You cannot stand that much of any one thing. And so it is with music. Any style of music that is all *tension* or all *relaxation* is sick music that will make you sick ... music that is all one or the other will not only affect you physically, it will affect you emotionally and spiritually as well.

(*The big beat:* Frank Garlock)

Already it should have become clear that there are certain principles to guide as to which music should be used in Christian meetings. We saw in Chapter 6 that the context in which words are used will affect the message those words convey, either to negate or to enforce it. The good news of the biblical message, if it is to have a musical context, surely warrants a *good* musical context?

Continual unvarying repetition of one strong, rhythm or of one chordal pattern, suggests a deathly monotony which is quite foreign to the gospel of abundant life; it is a way of numbing the God-given faculties of the mind, for the use of the mind in worship is an important biblical emphasis, ignored at our peril. And not without significance is the fact that such repetition of some phrase or action is the key to hypnosis.

As well as the danger of ceaseless repetition (and often linked with it) is the danger of the over-riding dominance of a steady, heavy, throbbing beat. One effect of music upon a person, as we have seen, can be physical: we want to put movement to it. And the kind of movements which are suggested by the stimulation of an insistent loud beat can easily become more sensual than spiritual if that physical reaction dominates a person's behaviour.

The effects of sheer loudness on the physical behaviour of the body's nervous system have already been noticed. Obviously the believer has no right to misuse the body by subjecting it to levels of noise that are harmful for the believer's body is the temple of the Holy Spirit, bought by the death of Christ. The reason for an unbeliever wanting music to be loud is usually because the noise is being used to drown out a sense of 'lostness' in life. Such music can be addictive — a drug, in fact.

A Reader in Personality at London University makes the point that one effect of certain kinds of 'pop' music can be to produce untypical and extravagant behaviour in the form of obsession and fantasizing:

> There is a third issue which explains this kind of behaviour in relation to pop music and that comes from the lights, special effects and trance-inducing music which can set up a hyp-notic effect. Through that people can lose an ordinary sense of judgement.
>
> (Quoted in *'Today'* newspaper, 19.9.95; De. Glenn Wilson)

Now it ought to be clear that no music which possesses any of the foregoing harmful influences can be a suitable companion for the biblical message in hymn or song. The Bible makes it clear that God's truth is essentially to be expressed in words. Any musical context must enhance the message of the words:

> Since in the wisdom of God the world through its wisdom did not know him, God was pleased through the foolishness of *what was preached* to save those who believe (*Italics mine* — HJA)
>
>   (1 Cor. 1:21, NIV).

Paul argues that the content of the gospel is essentially a verbal matter, something which is preached:

> We may say then that the definition of preaching which Paul is using here is: the declaration of words uncluttered by any concealing or confusing influence — the clear utterance of words ... they may be uttered to few at a time, or to many. They may be uttered in speech or in writing. They may be uttered in formal or informal circumstances or manners. But words there must be, and clarity there must be.
>   (*Music and communication of the gospel:* John Shakespeare, in a paper prepared for the Contemporary Christian Communication Seminar, 1977)

It follows that anything, whether it be music, personal behaviour, or incongruous surroundings, which muddles the clarity of the words of the gospel message must be offensive to the God whose gracious intention is that his message to mankind should be clearly verbalised.

Even though God communicated by signs and symbols in Old Testament times (and still communicates in the sacraments of baptism and the Lord's supper) nevertheless the spoken word always accompanies the signs in order to elucidate them. In his commentary on Exodus 33:19 Calvin indicates this principle:

> Although a vision was exhibited to his (Moses's) eyes the main point was in the voice; because true acquaintance with God is made more by the ears than by the eyes.

And in his comment on Isaiah 6:8 (as in a number of other places in his writings) Calvin emphasises this principle of the necessity of verbalising the message:

> Let us therefore learn that the chief part of the sacraments consists in the Word and without it they are absolute corruption. Figures are illusory without explanation.

The function of music, whether in congregational or in solo singing, must be to aid the clarity and sense of the words. The right music can express the emotional content of the words; it can, by its emphases, stress the meaning of the words; it can, by its appeal, draw out our affection to the words and fix them in our minds; at the very simplest, it can ensure that what is sung in a meeting is sung intelligibly because suitable music binds the many voices in the clarity of unison.

In all those ways right music can enhance a sense of worship; wrong music can destroy it. Moreover wrong music cannot be redeemed merely by combining it with right words since that creates confusion between the effect of the music and the message of the words. Can a diseased tree ever yield good fruit?

An interesting feature of Christian worship today is the advent of the 'song' as distinct from the 'hymn'. The difference between these two, as used nowadays, is probably not the distinction that the Apostle Paul made in Ephesians 5:19 — 'psalms, hymns and spiritual songs'. Charles Hodge suggests:

> *Psalmos* (psalm) was, agreeably to the etymology of the word, a song designed to be sung with the accompaniment of instrumental music ... a *humnos* (hymn) was a song of praise to God; a divine song ... *ode* (song) was religious or secular and therefore those here intended are described as 'spiritual' ... expressing spiritual thoughts and feelings.
>
> (*Commentary on Ephesians*)

As Hodge points out, a psalm was a hymn and a hymn was a song. There is however a clear distinction between the nature and purpose of hymns and songs as those terms are used today.

Hymns are compositions which seek to trace the development of some Bible truth and show its application to daily Christian life.

They are teaching tools; in the days of much illiteracy that was often one important purpose of their use. Consequently they tend to be longer than songs, to be relevant for much longer periods of time and to be shared more widely throughout the Christian world. They require considerable skill in composition.

The purpose of the song, on the other hand, is not so much to be a teaching tool as to be an expression of worship, adoration and devotion. It does not set out to teach or to develop a theme. The hymn, of course, can also be an expression of worship and love, but it is more than that whereas the song is simply that. Consequently the song is shorter, requiring less development in construction, making some brief and intense statement of personal devotion, as one might repeatedly declare one's love to a loved one. Often, because of its particular nature, the song is not tied to a tune of a normal metre (i.e. long metre, short metre, etc.). And that, in turn, may mean that its accompaniment will not be the traditional church organ!

The hymn often expresses what the Bible says to the Christian; the song expresses what the Christian feels towards God. The hymn speaks *about* God; the song speaks *to* God. And surely there is room for a balance of both those features in worship! The Christian meeting is not concerned only to stimulate the mind, but also to draw out the affection of the heart and the resolve of the will. Not one of those alone, but *a balance* of all three.

If it is true that the 'song' has emerged in Christian worship because of the influence of the charismatic movement, may we not say that it should in any case have come about because of the influence of Bible teaching? What is the value of a spiritual experience which is merely icily correct and splendidly regular? Can it not be that the expression of intense worship is, as A.W.Tozer suggested, the missing jewel of evangelicalism? Our Lord was able to commend the extravagant pouring out of the ointment over him from the broken alabaster pot and to defend the woman from the criticism of the coldly calculating disciples. It was an act of devotion which, in monetary terms, meant the equivalent of at least a whole year's wages poured out in one glorious blaze of love (Mark 14:3-9).

None of this is a justification for the unthinking, repetitive use of the song. There are bad songs which will rapidly disappear from use, as do bad hymns. And even the good song may well not have the durability of the good hymn as it may arise as a spontaneous expression of devotion related to some specific incident and will only be applicable in those moments of special (and perhaps unusual) devotion which are regrettably not as frequent as they ought to be. But that there is a place for the carefully chosen song used in a spirit of worship surely cannot be denied by any biblical rule.

There is a sense of music in heaven. For John heard a 'new song' and 'singing with a full voice' (Revelation 5:9,12), and a sound of 'harpists playing in their harps' (op.cit.14:2) singing a song which only the redeemed could learn. Whatever those symbols actually represent, in a book full of figurative language, they are plainly meaningless unless we are to understand a sense of music from them. If music can be acceptable in heaven then there can be right music on earth for the Christian and for Christian meetings. To find it is certainly a part of the responsibility of the Christian communicator.

In brief

Music has a powerful influence for good or ill; it must never be a matter of indifference.

To think about

'If you believe that churches are basically there to grow, you need to take seriously the fact that the only churches consistently growing are those which make an effort to inculturate their music'

(*Hymns and spiritual songs:* John Leach)

An attempt to offer a history of the development of 'pop' music and an examination of differences between it and 'classical' music appears in Appendix 4, as it may not be of general interest and does not directly concern the purpose of this chapter.

19.
The end — or is it the beginning?

Someone has said that it is impossible to step into a river in the same place twice: the stream will have moved on before the second time of your stepping in. In a similar way, the ways of our world are changing and changing increasingly rapidly. In one sense our horizons are continually widening as technology brings us new knowledge. In another sense our world is becoming smaller, for that same technology also brings the ends of the earth into our living rooms. Our world is also steadily becoming increasing complex: the simplicities of centuries ago are gone forever. Today's science is racing ahead of yesterday's ethics. Christian communicators with an unchanging message must learn how to present it in a continually changing society.

> All this means that Christians must go through a period of study, thought and re-evaluation that will take much of our energy. Conflicts will arise within Christian circles as older people especially are not consciously aware of this need for re-orientation, and therefore think that the old answers are still valid and sufficient. It is not that the foundation has to change, or that the basic doctrines have lost their meaning. But the expression and formulation of them sometimes needs re-thinking as we listen afresh to God's Word, and seek to present it to the new world in which we are living.
> (*Modern art and the death of a culture:* H.R.Rookmaaker)

That paragraph was written twenty-five years ago. How very relevant it still is today!

So there is no 'End' to the search for relevant and contemporary expressions of Christian worship and outreach. The task is on-going and continually urgent. The final page of this book is not an end of the search but should be regarded as a beginning. Certainly, the biblical revelation of God's truth and of his requirements is complete. It is not that new revelation is to be sought but the principles enshrined in that complete revelation must be extracted and continually applied relevantly to contemporary situations.

The applications of the same principles to differing situations will inevitably make the expression of them different. The principle of 'Safety First' was once expressed by a man with a red flag walking in front of the first motor cars. Today the same principle is expressed by traffic lights, white lines, zebra crossings, MOT tests, and driving tests. A man with a red flag would not last long on today's motorways.

History is valuable but not as something for us to preserve in all detail or to recreate in our day; neither should it make us long to have lived in the past rather than the present. Both those attitudes challenge the sovereign providence which has brought us into being today. History is for our learning: it shows us how the present has come about and warns us not to repeat its mistakes; it teaches us what God can do and confirms our trust in him. But it must not be our prison.

As we have seen, the society around us, in which a former culture based upon the Enlightenment view that human reason can bring about Utopia, is breaking down. The world is seen to be no nearer perfection than ever it was. Every benefit has a curse in it. The 'certainties' of the Enlightenment culture are yielding to the uncertainties of real life — Post-modernism. The task of confronting that collapsing culture with the certainties of God's message is hard but is the reason why God has appointed us to live here and now rather than at any other time in history. Our responsibility is to make the past Christian heritage relevant to present day needs. And for this we have the promised presence and work of the Holy Spirit who is the Spirit of knowledge (1 John 2:27). Our competence is from God (2 Cor. 3:5).

It is not for us to condemn, for God is the judge, but to pray and work for them (i.e. our non-Christian neighbours — HJA), meeting them openly and without reproach, accepting their ways and customs in the same way as Paul told us to be both Greek to the Greeks and Jew to the Jews. This means that we will have to study their problems, their ideas, know their language — what words mean to them — in order to be able to communicate.

(ibid.)

Charles Haddon Spurgeon, in his *Second series of lectures to my students*, raises the question of whether the essential aid of the Holy Spirit is obtained by abandoning all rational forms of study and coming to the pulpit with a blank mind. To answer that question Spurgeon recounts the following:

After a visitation discourse by the Bishop of Lichfield upon the necessity of earnestly studying the Word, a certain vicar told his lordship that he could not believe his doctrine, 'for', he said, 'often when I am in the vestry I do not know what I am going to talk about; but I go into the pulpit and preach, and think nothing of it'. His lordship replied, 'And you are quite right in thinking nothing of it, for your church wardens have told me that they share your opinion'.

We conclude where we began on the Dedicatory pages: the great question which Christian must keep permanently in their minds is: How can the ancient Scriptures continue to be the living voice of God for the present time?

This is your work; the Book is put in your hands to-day, that you may unfold its content to your people, conveying them into their minds by all possible avenues and applying them to all parts of their daily life.
(*The Yale lectures on preaching:* James Stalker, quoted in *toward an exegetical theology:* Walter C. Kaiser, Jnr.)

In brief

This book pleads for an understanding and application of those effective principles of communication with our fellows which were divinely designed and have been consistently used by the Triune God. To do so is a part of godliness.

Yet, even to do so will be inadequate without the Holy Spirit's life-giving energy. 'Do not quench the Spirit' (1 Thess. 5:19) either by discounting him or by ignoring his revealed ways of communicating.

To think about

'Where the Spirit of the Lord is, there is *eleutheria*' (2 Cor. 3:17).

> *eleutheria*: a — liberty to do or to omit things having no relation to salvation.
> (*Greek-English Lexicon:* Grimm/Thayer)

> *eleutheria*: The phraseology is that of manumission from slavery, which among the Greeks was effected by a legal fiction, according to which the manumitted slave was purchased by a god; as the slave could not provide the money, the master paid it into the temple Treasury in the presence of the slave, a document being drawn up containing the words 'for freedom'. *No one could enslave him again*, as he was the property of the god. (*Italics mine* — HJA)
> (*Expository Dictionary:* W.E.Vine)

The Matrix of Christian Witness

1. THE SPIRITUAL BARRENNESS OF OUR SECULAR AGE
A confused 'Christian message'
A multi-faith society developing
The all-pervasive atmosphere of secularism and materialism

2. THE POWER OF THE HOLY SPIRIT
The sovereign instrument of regeneration
The agent of illumination
Is not to be grieved, or quenched
Normally, uses the principles of communication

3. PRINCIPLES OF COMMUNICATION
Messages, not words, are communicated
Message = words plus context
Context established by relationship
Relationship = over-lapping frames of reference
What is understood is the message they thought you sent!

4. THE FLEXIBILITY OF N.T. MINISTRIES

*KERUSSO I herald, declare (dogmatic)
*EUANGELIZOMAI I bring good news (joyful)
DIDASKO I teach (cerebral)
PEITHO I persuade (emotional)
LALEO I talk (conversational)
DIALEGOMAI I reason (logical)

*ANGELLO I announce (commissioned)
MATHETEUO I instruct (discipling)
PARADIDOMAI I deliver-up (all-truth)
MARTUREO I testify (consistent life)
PARAKALEO I exhort (urgent)
GRAPHO I write (lasting)

The believer talks about The Faith from within these four situations, and needs to speak in a manner disciplined by all four.

---

*When these words are translated 'preach' in the A.V.
'it should be understood that "preaching" always means the proclamation of the Good News of God to the non-Christian world'.
(*The Translator's New Testament*: BFBS)

Appendix I

Extracts from a Theological Project of the World Evangelical Fellowship Communications Commission (Eight principles; from the report of a Study Conference hosted by the WEFCC, published 1984).

Principle 6. (by CHARLES H KRAFT)

God practises *Receptor orientated communication* by (among other things) showing respect for his receptors and the cultural, social, linguistic etc., frames of reference in which he finds them. We see it demonstrated over and over again in the Scriptures, that God chooses to employ human (rather than divine) language and culture, human geography, human homes and families etc., as the vehicles for interacting with human beings. We have no part of the biblical revelation in any but human language. Even when the concepts are difficult to understand (e.g. Jesus' parables, the book of Revelation) the language, analogies and all other materials from which the messages are built are completely human.

God makes himself dependent* on these vehicles both in the original communication of his messages and in their transmission and translation to successive generations of receptors. Indeed, he

---

*This dependency is not one of weakness but one of accommodation. Keep in mind that God in his all-wise providence fashioned the characters of his agents. He therefore knew that they would freely speak and write the words he wished to be written (HJA).

shows trust both in the vehicles and the humans who use them, in that (with the possible exception of the Ten Commandments) God did not himself record any of his revelation. As with Jesus and his disciples, he depended upon human beings to record what impressed them of his activities. This was under the guidance of God's Spirit, to be sure, but the vehicles were those of the receptors, not those of the source. This made them maximally understandable to those to whom they were directed (and to all succeeding generations.)

As I have said elsewhere (Kraft 1983:25) ... 'God employs our language and culture to get his ideas across to us, agreeing to the meanings that we attach to those symbols.

'Quite counter to God's example is that often found in the church. So often the church demands that would-be receptors learn a new vocabulary in order to understand what we are saying, so that the majority of the adjustment is on their part. We assume that they should learn our language, our customs, come to appreciate our kinds of music, come to our places of worship at our appointed times, adopt our lifestyles, associate with our kinds of people.

'This, of course, was what the early Jewish Christians assumed concerning the Gentiles. It is the approach that has come to be known as the heresy of the Judaizers. It was natural for them, and seems natural for us, to assume that those customs in terms of which God has met us are to be normative for all whom God meets ...'

Appendix II

Further extract from the World Evangelical Communication Commission Theological Project, (Eight Principles, published 1984.)

Principle 8. (KNUD JORGENSON)

God's way of communicating with man is basically *INCARNATIONAL*: even though he is above culture, he chooses to employ human culture and history as the arena of his interaction with man. This receptor orientation is evident throughout the entire biblical narrative. Thus he comes to Israel from within its world-view and through its history, employing its human vehicles of communication and using its frame of reference — even when that frame of reference is coloured by Canaanite culture. And just as Israel learned to know God from history and culture, it also talked about him in the forms of history and culture. As a result the Bible should be viewed as an inspired classic casebook and not as a generalised textbook.

The climax of God's incarnational communication is based in his dwelling among us in Jesus Christ: in the fullness of time God communicates himself, in the person of his Son in whom the Word became a human being. Here God encoded his infinite qualities in the limitations of human language and human form. And by so doing, he broke through all our stereotypes and bridged the gap between his supercultural realm and culture-bound humanity.

As Christ-communicators, we are called to model our communication on God's incarnational approach. This means that communication of the incarnation must be incarnate in the contemporary world's language, history and cultures: Christ must take form in ever new communication settings and contexts.

Confronted with this task and the great diversity of contexts into which the Good news is to be communicated, we need to distinguish between the supracultural/normative content and meanings of the Bible and their culture-bound interpretations. This requires a thorough knowledge of the cultural contexts of the Bible, of our own context and of the context of the receiver. This knowledge should in turn lead us into a dialogue between the questions and felt-needs of the receiver and answers of Scripture. The aim of this dialogue is a continuous mutual engagement between the horizons of the Biblical texts and the horizons of the receptor culture. Basic to this dialogue between the Biblical texts and the receptor culture, is the belief that God's incarnational approach to communication/revelation makes it clear that we can only know his word as a message contextualised in a particular culture.

In this process of Christ taking form in ever new settings, every new proclamation in a new socio-cultural context will result is partial newness of meaning. Such new proclamation and new meanings are to be measured against the Biblical yardstick, and must fall within the Bible's own range of acceptable variation. That means that any proclamation of Christ in a new setting must be anchored in the Biblical framework. The primary aim of this incarnational process is *dynamic equivalence:* to communicate the Biblical message in such a way that it produces an impact on contemporary hearers equivalent to that which it produced on the original hearers. *The primary author of such a dynamic equivalent message is the Holy Spirit, who bears witness to Christ and thus affects a kind of extension of the incarnation. (Italics mine — HJA)*

Appendix III

It is a useful study to compare the style of the editorial comments in different newspapers, when they are all concerned with the same issue. The style of writing used for example in 'The Sun' or 'The Daily Mirror' is quite different from that used by 'The Daily Telegraph' or 'The Times'. The Christian communicator meets both 'Mirror' and 'Times' readers; if those papers have worked out an appropriate style for their readers, can the Christian communicator be wise in ignoring their insights?

> In most newspaper offices there is to be found a manual known as a style book, which lays down, for the sake of consistency, the paper's rules on the usage of words and punctuation.
> (*The Mirror's way with words:* Keith Waterhouse)

On Friday, May 13th, 1994, commenting upon the sudden death of John Smith, Leader of the Labour party, *The Times* wrote:

> Much of the Opposition's loss is clear enough already. Yesterday's tributes, led by the Prime Minister's gracious statement to the Commons, were a powerful representation of what has now gone. John Smith epitomised the virtues of decency, vigour and authority, which, well used, can turn politicking into statesmanship. He was, as Tennyson wrote of Wellington, 'rich in saving common-sense'; unlike the fallen duke, he will never have a chance to be 'the foremost captain of his time'. It was a chance he richly deserved.

On the same day *The Sun* commented, under the headline — 'Nation robbed of a man who would be king':

John Smith was a good man. The kind you would be proud to have as your neighbour. A man without an ounce of malice in him. He was the bank manager you trust, the safe pair of hands, the wise old friend whose advice you rely on.

The contrast between the two editorial comments ought to be instructive. It could be good for the serious Christian sometimes to read a variety of newspapers in order to study their various styles of spreading their news. Editors write in order to attract readers; should not the Christian communicator be equally determined to attract hearers?

In 1995 John Major resigned and offered himself in an election for the Leader of the Conservative party, in order to test whether he had the confidence of the party or not. He won. On Wednesday July 5th *The Daily Mirror* commented:

John Major has got what he wanted. But only up to a point. He remains Prime Minister and Leader of the Conservative Party. But only up to a point. Tory MPs have demonstrated that they back him. But only up to a point. The Leadership election proved that the Conservatives are deeply divided. We knew that, though.

Whereas *The Times* expresses its opinions in quite a different style:

When Mr Major made his sudden announcement of this contest two weeks ago *The Times* did not join in the chorus of those who applauded his courageous move. We called his coup a *coup de theatre*; and so it proved until the end. Only the presentation yesterday was a success. Only the most credulous in the party could see the Prime Minister's rejection by one third of his MPs as a triumph.

The point of making these comparisons has nothing to do with the particular political stance of the papers, but simply to offer a way of analysing the manner in which they expressed their views. A careful analysis even of these brief examples will revel several differences in style from which the Christian can surely learn. It is sad when:

... the children of this age are more shrewed in dealing with their own generation than are the children of light

(Luke 16:8).

Appendix IV

It cannot have escaped anyone's notice that there are two kinds of music in our Western world culture: classical and so called 'pop'. To define the difference between the two is not a simple task. 'Pop' must mean more than 'popular' (though it is that) because there is classical music which is very popular (witness the success of Classic FM broadcasts). And classical music is not all of one sort — there is the Baroque period, the Romantic period, the Modern period, etc.

The answer to the question, How did this split in the kinds of music arise? It may perhaps help us to identify the difference between them. The roots of 'pop' music have an identifiable beginning. Rookmaaker makes the point that:

> in the seventeenth and eighteenth centuries, before the deep, dissolving effects of the Enlightenment became apparent, there was a unity in the whole culture. As far as music was concerned there were different streams ... church music, or opera, chamber music, dance music, and many more. But there was no break in society. ... There was a sense of normality and genuineness about all this music that made it everybody's music, ... The nineteenth century made music into a kind of refined, cultural, almost pseudo-religious revelation of humanism ... The twentieth century made the split complete, particularly with the advent of modern music, with its weird sounds and lack of consonance.
>
> (*Modern art and the death of a culture*: H.R.Rookmaaker)

'Pop' music may therefore be understood as a style of music which defines a cultural era, beginning in the mid-to-late nineteenth century and still evolving today. And that process of evolution, which began with music designed as a protest against the hypocrisy and shallowness (as it was seen) of the traditional society of that time, has developed into what Rookmaaker calls 'a neo-paganistic primitivism' in which the words, as well as the message, of the music can descend to thinly disguised calls to sensuality, drugs and violent protest. A former music critic of '*The Observer*' writes:

> Elvis' style was impossible to define. He sang country, gospel, rhythm, blues and pop — all mixed into one ... The only constants were sex and excitement ... He came on leering and twitching, his hair all down in his eyes, his grin lop-sided. The moment the music started, he went berserk. Spasms rocked his body as if it had been plugged into the same electrical source as his guitar. His hips began to grind, his legs vibrated. He pouted and humped and walked as if he were sneering with his legs. On stage, he bounded like a jeep driver crossing a ploughed field. On TV, sponsors would allow Presley to be shown only from the waist up.
>
> (*All you need is love:* Tony Palmer)

There was deliberate sensuality. For other singers drugs and violence are not far away; for example:

> One pill makes you larger
> And one pill makes you small;
> But the ones that mother gives you
> Don't do anything at all —
> Go ask Alice
> When she's ten feet tall.
>
> (from '*White Rabbit*' by Jefferson Airplane)

> Everywhere I hear the sound of marching feet, boy
> 'Cause summer's here and the time is right for fighting in the street, boy.
>
> (*Street Fighting Man:* The Rolling Stones)

Of the Rolling Stones Tony Russell writes:

> They were the eccentric, threatening extreme of British pop in the sixties, and the chief spokesman of swinging, liberated, promiscuous London.
>
> (*St Michael Encyclopaedia of Rock:* Tony Russell, Ed.)

Yet the discerning ear can sometimes hear within the 'pop' scene expressions of human longings which are common to us all, if perhaps more so to youth than to the aged. 'Pop' lyrics sometimes contain a real cry for help to which the Christian communicator ought to listen — it is often the voice of the unbeliever, seeking for answers to his or her questions. And Tony Russell goes on to make the point concerning The Beatles (1958-71, contemporary with the Rolling Stones) that:

> To both parents and the younger record buyer, the Beatles represented the other, safer and more melodic extreme.
>
>   (ibid.)

Of their songs, Dave Rogers comments (? prophetically):

> the Beatles (taken as a group and as individuals after the break-up of the group) ... added to what must in the final analysis be seen as one of the finest bodies of popular song of the century.
>
>   (*Pop music in schools:* Vulliamy and Lee, Ed.)

Moreover, there have been several instances where 'pop' music has been the medium which has harnessed unprecedented flows of charity for humanitarian causes. In 1967, the first worldwide television link broadcasting to more than 400 million people when the Beatles song 'All you need is love' was the highlight; in 1971, George Harrison master-minded the Concert for Bangladesh which raised large financial relief for that stricken country; 'pop' star Bob Geldhof enlisted the help of many 'superstars' to raise money for famine relief in Ethiopia. The 'hit' song of that event was 'Do they know it's Christmas?', the recording of which became the biggest selling single ever, with sales in excess of 3 million.

Most famously, the Live Aid concert which followed in July 1985, comprising simultaneous concerts in London and Philadelphia, was witnessed by:

> ... an estimated 2,000 million people across the world, with telethons and associated campaigns in 22 countries raising of $70 million. Such was the enormous success of the venture many subsequent fund raising-events took their lead from Live Aid.
>
>   (*The wild guide to rock:* Michael Horsham/David McCarthy)

Quite evidently, not all 'pop' music is to be dismissed as depraved and corrupting even though the 'pop' scene is so often soiled by those who have succumbed in the temptations of promiscuity, drugs, alcohol and suicide. The name of Cliff Richards (b. 1941) is still prominent in the rock scene, yet he is known as an evangelical Christian. Evidently he does not find any incongruity between his faith and his singing. The hard task is to identify what is good and what is bad, what is a true cry of human need and what is a deliberate expression of unbridled lust. This matter of evaluation is such a difficult question to answer.

'Pop' must not be judged using the criteria by which we judge classical music. Classical music, which arose in the Middle Ages and has developed until the present, is rooted in a Western Europe which was largely isolated from the rest of the world*. But as the world has steadily become 'a global village', 'pop' has emerged as a cross-fertilisation of multi-cultural styles, resulting in an international musical eclecticism. 'Pop' is an amalgam of such styles as jazz, blues, gospel, folk, country and western, boogie-woogie, soul, reggae, rock'n'roll, skiffle, beat and more!

Without going into detailed definitions of these terms, the point is obvious: classical music developed in isolation from the rest of the world; 'pop' by a fusion of styles from various parts of the world — Indian, African, Southern USA (slavery and after), American Gospel singing, Ras Tafarian, etc. Nor must we overlook the fact that 'pop' performances have so often been made extravagant by the pressure of commercial necessity for such musical events to become competitive, spectacular entertainments with 'stars' as idols.

'Pop' music is mainly music by young people for young people; its 'idols' are necessary because they:

> personified the fantasies, aspirations and rebelliousness of an adolescent audience ... It is its immediacy, rough edges and integrity which gives a good pop song its meaning, feeling and universality ... Youth styles, modes of dress and

---

* The style of church music has likewise, until now, developed in isolation from non-European music. The Gregorian chant was only melody. From Reformation times the hymn tune combined melody, harmony and rhythm in balance. But now there is a predominant emphasis upon rhythm in new Christian songs resulting from wider influences of otherworld cultures. We have swung from melody alone to emphatic rhythm.

behaviour, stances towards authority and one another, are all
inextricably linked in its meaning.

(*Pop music in school:* Vulliamy and Lee, Ed.)

There is a very real sense in which we have got what we asked for,
in the emergence and development of the 'Pop Era'. It was a
nominally 'Christian' Europe which cruelly dragged Africans as
slaves to the plantations of the West Indies and America. Their
consequent African work-songs and spirituals were, not unnatu-
rally, alive with a hope for a *better* land. Drums were forbidden,
because they could be used for sending messages. The rhythm had
to be all in the longing of the voice and the haunting melodies.

After black emancipation, the intransigence of white (?'Christian') society to permit real integration led to the creation of blues
music and marching music (for freedom had not brought its expected benefits), which in turn led to the use of portable instruments
and drums which could be played while marching. Riding rail-cars
(without tickets) from city to city in search of work led to the
introduction of boogie woogie whose repetitive bass rhythm reproduced the rhythm of the train wheels on the rail tracks.

Unwelcome in white circles, black musicians were confined to
work brothels and clubs which were frequently run by those of
mixed Creole race who had, since the emancipation of blacks, been
pushed out of white (?'Christian') society. It may even be that the
very term 'jazz' derived from this source, since the Southern drawl
of the United States referred to prostitutes as 'jazz-belles' (a
corruption of 'jezebels'). From the rhythmic and exciting variations
of the old tunes that they knew came official jazz and rag-time. It fell
to Scott Joplin (1868-1917) to rescue rag-time from such dubious
surroundings and to make it respectable for a wider, even white,
society to enjoy.

Curiously, Christian churches in America provided the example
and impetus for singing to become a dramatic performance by their
Gospel singers. A significant number of those who subsequently
became 'Rock stars' began as Gospel singers.

Testifying to the Lord was a moment of abandon; emotional
display in church was a sign of devotion. The greater the
display, the greater the supposed devotion ... they might
seem possessed as they howled and wept ... passion had
become a style and a necessity.

(*All you need is love:* Tony Palmer)

Gospel singing came to have a gripping excitement and the secular scene rapidly grasped the value of that for commercial success. And now modern technology provides the means for 'pop' concerts to be spectacular, sometimes outrageous displays which inflame audience emotions. And it all began in church!

This has, inevitably, been a very simplified survey of a complex subject, described much more fully in such titles as Tony Palmer's '*All you need is love: the story of popular music*', from which some of the information presented here has been drawn; information which perhaps will be a helpful basis for forming opinions. Ignorant judgements are unwise judgements; it was just one such ignorant judgement which wickedly put Jesus Christ on the cross.

Appendix V

Extracts from a helpful guide to those with opportunity to use radio broadcasts, on hospital radio, local or community radio stations, published by Grace Baptist Mission, 12 Abbey Close, Abingdon, OX14 3JD.

General Notes

Find out the attitude of the station to religious broadcasting. Some stations allow a more positive approach than others. Some stations ask for a live talk; others demand pre-recording, sometimes several weeks in advance. The advantage of the live talk is that there is the opportunity to use current themes. In the case of pre-recorded talks, avoid themes which are dated, such as Christmas and New Year, unless specifically asked for them.

Length

Even a one minute or one and a half minute slot can be used as a signpost, pointing people in a direction they might not otherwise consider. Be careful to keep to the allotted time. You may not be asked again if you take too long!

Context

Know the context of your talk — will it be within a secular new programme or a religious magazine programme? What time of day is it? Who is likely to be listening? What age? What culture/ education?

The message

The message is best centred on the life which Jesus Christ enables us to live and the benefits of trusting in him, rather than on sin and salvation. This is not to deny the gospel, nor to exclude such matters altogether, but it is to say that our 'pagan' listeners will more readily understand what we are trying to say, if we talk about a person rather than theology.

Approaching the message

One person's experience is totally different from another's. Look for something that you might have in common with your listener, e.g. love of sport, gardening, a mutual friend or acquaintance, children, topical issues. Always move from the *known* to the *unknown*. An indirect approach is not the same as saying nothing. We dare not use the opportunity given without a positive message. The indirect approach seeks to begin with something that people relate to and possibly approve of. Or try something personal. Keep a scrap-book with anything that comes to mind about day to day issues, quotations, incidents, etc., that can be used in an indirect approach.

Writing

Type your script (if possible) in double spacing, with a large left-hand margin to allow for last minute corrections, and for ease of reading. Careful fine tuning of a script will make it possible for us to say something worthwhile. Every unnecessary word or phrase must be deleted, but the result must not be so terse as to be harsh on the ear. You may have to restore some deleted words so as to 'oil the works'. Aim at an introduction which will gain people's attention — if a story, then start straight with the action; or start with a witty remark, or thought-provoking question or statement. Aim at a quick conclusion — probably the last sentence or two, applying the message to the listener.

Direct Scripture quotations should be kept to a minimum. (Paul had none in his Mars Hill sermon — Acts 17:16-31.) If you do use one, make sure it will be clearly understood by those unfamiliar with Bible language.

Write too much to start with. Try to make your script something you'd say spontaneously. Contractions are common in spoken language — use them. But sometimes a contraction can destroy an emphasis — "Christianity has not been tried" ... needs the emphasis on *not*, while "hasn't" would be in danger of losing the emphasis.

Don't be afraid of ending the sentence on a preposition — in normal speech this is often what we do end with! Also, start sentences with 'And' or 'But', when this is natural. Use short words — don't try to impress the listener. Use short sentences; (average about 11 words). Cut out needless words. Mix them up — follow a longer sentence by two shorter ones. Use verbs rather than nouns — verbs create action and excitement, and make reading lively and interesting. Use direct speech. This is more interesting than long descriptions. Write as you would talk to a friend, and the listener will feel you are his friend. *Rewrite* — rewrite — rewrite ...

Presentation

Practise thoroughly! Rehearse again and again for fine tuning and timing. Any words or phrases you stumble over in rehearsal should be resolutely changed even if they were something you were very proud of. Practise reading in different ways — in a friendly manner, sincerely, a conversational manner. Read it very, very slowly so that every sound in every word comes out. Underline important words. Read it again at normal speed. Be yourself. Speak one to one. *Smile* — sit comfortably — relax — smile — yawn — stretch — smile — speak to a friend sitting just in front of you. (In fact, a smile can be 'heard' on radio.) Practise pacing the talk — vary the speed, tone and emphasis.

Put expression into your presentation. *Do not shout* — neither be very quiet. Use pitch and tone for emphasis. Shouting does not mean convincing! If you shout at me you don't really care about me. Speak with authority and confidence. This makes the information believable. Check your pronunciation. Bad pronunciation means your talk will lack authority. Light humour is good on radio if you do it well. When you do, enjoy it yourself by a smile on your face and by letting a natural chuckle come into your voice. Practise the chuckle!

Bibliography

Titles of books from my bookshelf which have been helpful — some more than others — during the preparation of this book. Not all are from Evangelical writers; some are secular studies. A number may now be out of print since they were obtained a long time ago.

Adams, J E	*Studies in Preaching*	Presby. & Reformed
Barclay, W	*Communicating the Gospel*	St Andrews Press
Bavinck, J H	*Introduction to the Science of Missions*	Presby. & Reformed
Beekman/Callow	*Translating the Word of God*	Zondervan
Benington, J	*Culture, Class & Christian belief*	Scripture Union
Bruce, F F	*The Apostolic Defence of the Gospel*	IVP
Carnell, E J	*An Introduction to Christian Apologetics*	Eerdmans
Clowney, E P	*Preaching & Biblical Theology*	Tyndale Press
Conn, H M	*Contemporary World Theology*	Presby. & Reformed
Creighton, J E	*An Introductory Logic*	Macmillan
Duthie, A S	*Bible translations & how to chose between them*	Paternoster
Garlock, F	*The Big Beat*	Bob Jones University
Godet, F L	*Defence of the Christian Faith*	T & T Clark
Green, M	*Evangelism in the Early Church*	Hodder & Stouhton
Hall, S (Ed.)	*Formations of Modernity*	Open University
Heimbeck, R S	*Theology & Meaning*	Allen & Unwin

Hesslegrave, D J	*Communicating Christ Cross-culturally*	Zondervan
Horsham, M and McCarthy, D	*The wild guide to rock*	Quintet Publishing
Kaiser, W C (Jnr)	*Toward an Exegetical Theology*	Baker
Leach, J	*Hymns and Spiritual Songs*	Grove Books
Lee, F	*The central significance of culture*	Presby. & Reformed
Lewis, C S	*The Abolition of Man*	Collins/Fount
Lewis, G R	*Testing Christianity's Truth claims*	Moody Press
Marston, G W	*The Voice of Authority*	Ross House Books
Mares, C	*Teach yourself communication*	E.U.P.
Masters, P	*Biblical strategies for witness*	Wakeman
Mayers, M K	*Christianity confronts culture*	Zondervan
McGrath, A	*Bridge Building*	IVP
Murray, J	*Collected Writings, Vol 1*	Banner of Truth
Palmer, T	*All you need is love (the story of popular music)*	Futura Publications
Perry, M	*Preparing for worship*	Marshall Pickering
Prior, K F W	*The Gospel in a Pagan Society*	Hodder & Stoughton
Ramm, B	*Protestant Christian Evidences*	Moody Press
Robinson, M N	*Biblical Preaching*	Baker Book House
Rookmaaker, H R	*Modern Art & the Death of a Culture*	Appollos (IVP)
Rowe, T	*The Communication Process*	Epworth Press
Russell, T (Ed.)	*St Michael Encyclopaedia of Rock*	Octopus Books
Schaeffer, F	*The God Who Is There*	Hodder & Stoughton
Scholes, P A	*The Puritans & Music*	Oxford Clarendon
Schramm, W	*The Process & Effects of Mass Communication*	University of Illinois
Stonehouse, N B	*Paul before The Areopagus*	Presby. & Reformed
Swinburne, R	*The Existence of God*	Clarendon Press
Till, C Van	*Defence of the Faith*	Presby. & Reformed
Valliamy, G (Ed. Lee)	*Pop music in school*	Cambridge Univ. Press
Walker, A	*Enemy Territory*	Hodder & Stoughton
Ward, K	*The battle for the soul*	Hodder & Stoughton
Waterhouse, K	*The Mirror's way with Words*	Mirror Books
Watts/Williams	*The Psychology of Religious Knowing*	Geoffrey Chapman

Wells, D F	*God in the Wasteland*	IVP
	No place for truth	Eerdmans
Williamson, P	*Christianity confronts Modernity*	Handsel Press
Winter, B W	*Seek the Welfare of the City*	Paternoster
	The translator's New Testament	B & F Bible Society